LUNDIE'S STORIES

Tales from a Wyoming Original

LUNDIE'S STORIES

Tales from a Wyoming Original

Lundie Thayer
Karen King

Library of Congress Control Number: 2019913802
ISBN: Hardcover   978-1-7960-5875-8
                 Softcover   978-1-7960-5874-1
                 eBook   978-1-7960-5873-4

FRONT COVER PICTURE: Annie, Lundie, and Sid Thayer, c. 1918 with the orphaned ram that was given a quart of milk every day. *(Thayer family photo)*

Print information available on the last page.

Rev. date: 09/24/2019

To order additional copies of this book, contact:
Xlibris
1-888-795-4274
www.Xlibris.com
Orders@Xlibris.com
798039

CONTENTS

Notes From The Authors vii

Chapter 1   Family 1
Chapter 2   Animals 44
Chapter 3   Weather 72
Chapter 4   Military 83
Chapter 5   Employment 96
Chapter 6   Gardening 108
Chapter 7   Places 114
Chapter 8   Cures 126
Chapter 9   Politics 131
Chapter 10   Characters 140
Chapter 11   Advice 175

Epilogue 177

NOTES FROM THE AUTHORS

Although my dad, Donald J. King Sr., was born in Lander, Wyoming, in 1921 and I've lived in Fremont County for more than 40 years, I'm still a Colorado transplant compared to Lundie, a true Wyoming original who descended as a fourth-generation pioneer with lineage in Wyoming dating back to the mid-1800s and his great-grandmother's sojourn from England to the Greybull River. Lundie and Doris Thayer were my friends since 1992, giving me opportunity to personally witness a few of the events shared on these pages. Whether fact or fiction, these stories were told to me while Lundie and I sat on his couch he called a "davanaugh" from January 15 to August 2, 2015, which was an entertaining way to pass a long Wyoming winter, rainy spring, and hot summer.

Together, we laughed often and cried a few times. Together, we thought about the categories and decided they would help us stay organized instead of trying to remember everything in chronological order. We kept notes in each category where Lundie wrote key words that triggered his memory for the full story. Then Lundie would tell me the story as I typed it into a laptop.

Writing LUNDIE'S STORIES was truly an honor that could have easily reached one thousand pages. The story of Doris, age 85, and Lundie, age 88, helping me build a porch is not included. The story of Lundie bringing a round and long rattle snake toward me all the while telling me it's dead until he shakes it right beside me like it's alive did not make this collection. Believe me, there are many more Lundie stories, which is why at least a few of them had to be written. Working with such a living legend was a real treat few people experience. Even at 100 years old, Lundie's mind was clear and exact as verified in the following tales. I hope you enjoy his stories and a glimpse of old Wyoming from a man who lived through astounding times that will never return.

Karen King, Fort Washakie, Wyoming

KKing

Meeteetse Creek Cemetery, Grannie Speck's (Amelia Cunningham) tombstone. George Thayer hauled the marble stone on his freight wagon from the Cody Train Depot to the cemetery, more than 30 miles. *(Karen King photo)*

DEDICATED TO
GRANNIE SPECKS

I like to be honest, so I definitely want to credit my great-grandmother, Amelia Spencer, from England. She is buried at the Meeteetse Creek Cemetery. I knew her only as Grannie Specks, who homesteaded in the area. Grannie's first husband was named Robert Fenton, and she named Fenton, Wyoming, for him before 1870. Grannie Specks was born in Beckingham, England, on January 21, 1835, and died on August 27, 1911, in Fenton, Wyoming, at the age of 76 years, seven months and six days. Her courage to travel by horse and wagon with four little children across the wild, open spaces between Oregon, Missouri, and Salt Lake City, Utah, is something to admire.

Lundie Thayer

CHAPTER 1

Family

Now, I can't personally know about all this 'cuz I wasn't even born yet, but I'll try to tell you what I remember my folks tellin' me about the past. All my life, I heard these stories when my grandparents, mother, and father were alive. I don't remember the dates if I ever knew them, but I'll be honest with you the best I can remember.

My grandmother, Annie, told me about my great-grandmother named Grannie Specks. She got the name 'cuz she used a monocle to read but always wore a pair of glasses to do other chores. It's pretty impressive that she could read at all back in those days.

Anyway, Grannie Specks came from around Piccadilly, England. I remember that name 'cuz it sounds so funny. Her real name was Amelia Spencer, and she married a man named Fenton. They had four children when Fenton was run over by a milk wagon in England. The children's names were Bob, Fannie, Jack, and Annie. Grannie Specks was a cook for Queen Victoria around 1867. The queen had to give permission to Grannie Specks to migrate to the United States, and her brother-in-law sent her money from Utah for the passage. She came to the United States with the children on the steamship *Wyoming*, which took about 36 days to arrive on Ellis Island. My grandmother, Annie, was just a baby when they got to the United States.

I think Grannie Specks came by railroad to the Missouri River 'cuz they were workin' on the Union Pacific railroad, "The Golden Spike," then. The train from New York carried Grannie Specks and the kids to Oregon, Missouri. From there, she came by covered wagon to Utah.

Along the way to Salt Lake City, Fannie got tick fever and died around 1869 at the age of six or seven while the country was still grievin' the assassination of Abraham Lincoln. The wagon master left Grannie Specks and the kids along the trail but said he'd send help so they could catch up later with the wagon train. Well, the help was seven Indians. Grannie Specks thought the family was gonna be killed for sure when they saw their help ridin' up. Bob and Grannie had a shotgun but didn't shoot it 'cuz the leader of the Indian group held his hand up in peace. The Fox Indians helped bury Fannie along the Oregon Trail, probably somewhere in Nebraska.

Later, when Grannie Specks rejoined the wagon train, she found out a Fox Indian's story. As a baby, the Fox Indian's family tied him to a log and threw him in the Missouri River where a white man on a ferry crossing the river grabbed a rope, jumped in the river, and saved the baby. The white man's family raised the Fox Indian to adulthood and taught him to speak English, which really helped Grannie Specks to bury Fannie years later. The Fox Indian was a scout for the U.S. Cavalry and probably saved Grannie Specks' whole family when he helped them catch up with the wagon train and continue westward.

I think my grandma, Annie, told me it took approximately six weeks to reach Salt Lake. When they arrived in Salt Lake City, Utah, Grannie Specks' brother-in-law, I think his name was John Fenton, wanted her to become his seventh wife and live in Utah. Grannie Specks wouldn't agree to that arrangement.

She got to talkin' to another man and his wife in Salt Lake. She liked the name "Wyoming," like the steamship that brought her from England. The man mentioned it several times sayin' that in Wyoming there was a Greybull River with plenty of land and water open to homesteaders. The couple helped her get a wagon, team, and one cow, along with supplies to go to Wyoming. After fourteen days, she and the family arrived in the area along the Greybull River where only a few other people lived. She named her homestead Fenton, Wyoming, after her English husband, Robert.

At that time, homesteads were different. The government issued "land grants" for 640 acres, which was a section of land. After Wyoming became a state in 1890, the government changed land grants to homesteads of 640 acres.

The family lived in a dugout and Grannie Specks established a post office in Fenton. She helped cowboys and other workers order supplies from a Montgomery Ward catalog, which was the only way to get supplies there. Oftentimes, the supplies weren't delivered for at least a year while mail came in and went out only twice, every six months. No schools were available, so Grannie Specks taught her own children to read and do arithmetic. The family had their own livin' right there on the homestead. The nearest neighbor was named Alec Roach, who lived up the river from where Grannie Specks settled. The only cow she had was bred by Roach's bull and delivered a single bull calf. That became the bull for the rest of the cows she raised. Since there were no fences at the time, only rock corner posts that marked property, you can imagine how hard it was to keep a bull around.

A good story about Alec Roach was when he accused Grannie Specks and Bob of stealin' all the irrigating water out of the Greybull River. The only trouble was that Roach lived upriver from Grannie Speck's homestead. My grandmother told me he was pretty fuzzy and this incident surely proved it. Well, Grannie Specks and Bob had dug the ditches themselves with the help of the team they brought from Salt Lake. Part of the Fenton homestead was right along the river, just like Roach's, so Grannie Specks figured she'd help Mr. Roach anyway. She sent Bob up to the Roach place to give him a hand with his water problem.

Bob jumped on a horse bareback and went to the Roach place. When he got there, he could hear Mr. Roach beatin' somethin' up inside the chicken coop, yellin', "Take that, Bob! Take that!"

But Bob was sittin' on his horse outside. Since he was just a boy, he got scared and took off toward home. When he told Grannie Specks what he heard, she told him, "OK, let him fix his own water."

As time went by and things became more peaceful, Mr. Roach arrived at the post office one day and wanted to order from the catalog. Grannie Specks went through the catalog with him and arrived at a page where he pointed and said, "I want that."

Grannie Specks didn't understand what he wanted, so she asked him, "Are you going to wear dresses?"

Mr. Roach replied, "Hell, no. I want what's in the dress."

That's the God's truth, as my grandma told me so.

Back then, there was a magazine called *Heart and Hand*, which was like a flyer in the Montgomery Ward catalog advertising a chance to meet the opposite sex. Grannie Specks felt sorry for Mr. Roach, so she showed him a copy of *Heart and Hand*. Mr. Roach got excited about meetin' a lady, but he couldn't read or write, only look at the pictures. So Grannie Specks wrote love letters to a lady in Chicago on behalf of Mr. Roach.

As time went by, the Chicago lady showed up on the Greybull wantin' to know where Alec Roach lived. Grannie Specks had to tell the truth to the lady and explained that she wasn't Alec Roach, but she did write letters and "made love" through the mail. The lady still wanted to meet Mr. Roach, so Grannie Specks offered to take her to the Roach place. Bob rode up to the Roach's and told Mr. Roach the lady was at their homestead. Mr. Roach decided to come down to the Fenton Post Office and met the lady from Chicago.

Later that day, the lady asked Grannie Specks if she could spend the night with them in Fenton 'cuz she wanted to see Mr. Roach again. Well, as the story goes, Mr. Roach went back to Chicago with the lady and instructed Grannie Specks to sell off the Roach property, livestock, and the homestead until they came back to Wyoming or sent further word. After a few years, Mr. Roach and the lady did come back to Fenton.

My grandma said there was no finer man in the whole Wyoming Territory. He was well-dressed, had a slick haircut, shiny shoes, and talked fancy. Somewhere along the line, Mr. Roach and the lady got married and invested in the stock market where they made a killin', so Mr. Roach had no worries anymore about water or anything else.

The livestock went to other pioneers migratin' through the area and Grannie Specks asked to buy the Roach homestead. The Roaches wanted $1 an acre, which no one would pay in them days. Grannie Specks offered 50¢ an acre to the Roaches. 'cuz Grannie Specks had been honest in sellin' the other Roach property and livestock, the Roaches agreed to accept the $320 for 640 acres.

An adventure happened later on the Fenton place when a man come ridin' in on a horse, fell off and couldn't get back on. Uncle Bob and Grannie Specks put the unknown man in a wheelbarrow and hauled him to the dugout, their home. His leg was swollen up with poison by a rattle snake bite. As luck would have it, Doc Kenney came ridin' in. Doc Kenney was a vet and a doctor too, which was really lucky for the man. When he saw the swollen leg, Doc Kenney said the only thing to do was amputate it and asked Grannie Specks if she had a meat saw and some whiskey. They had to get the man drunk to cut off the leg. Grannie Specks had three-quarters of a quart of whiskey that she used to doctor the kids if needed. That wasn't enough to take a leg off, so she sent Bob down to Polleys, a neighbor about three miles away, to see if they had any whiskey. The Polleys had two quarts that they sent back with Bob. Then Doc Kenney told Bob and Jack to go out and find a green branch of cottonwood that he could use to plug the end of the man's leg bone.

The boys came back with a green branch that Doc Kenney whittled into the right-sized plug. The man drank every drop of the whiskey and passed out. Doc Kenney took the meat saw and amputated the leg. My grandma Annie told me the man would scream a little bit and then pass out again right away. They kept givin' him whiskey to get through the surgery. The plug was used and Doc Kenney took the flesh and pulled it back over the bone before he sewed the skin up with catgut that was used on animals too 'cuz catgut would disintegrate as the wound healed.

Doc Kenney stayed in the bunkhouse that night 'cuz Grannie Specks had a sick horse too which he took care of the next day. Doc Kenney loaded up his pack horse and saddle horse to ride out when he said, "He's not gonna make it. So just dig a hole and bury him 'cuz we don't even know his name. Just bury him, and we won't need a death certificate." Then Doc Kenney rode off.

Well, Grannie Specks nursed the man's leg for six months, got him back on one foot and took him for rides in the wheelbarrow. Doc Kenney come ridin' in one day, walked into the house and there sat his patient, alive with only one leg. About a year later, Grannie Specks received $100, which was a lot of money, from the one-legged man who by then had moved to Billings, Montana.

Bob and Jack grew up on the Fenton homestead with Grannie Specks and never moved away. Jack never married. Bob always said he'd never marry anyone and didn't until late in life. Maybe he didn't know how to train a woman, but Bob could look at a dog and train it to do anything—anything!

A woman brought him a little female Cocker Spaniel to train and then came back to see how her dog's training was going. Bob told her, "Everything's fine. Watch this."

He told the dog to show her how the girls lay in the morning. The dog rolled over on her back and stuck all four legs straight in the air. The woman was disgusted and thought Bob had taught her dog filth. She threatened to take him to court, but the judge wouldn't even consider that case. Bob surely did meet the judge later.

Judge Metz had heard a story about Bob burnin' the Kaiser. It seems that after WWI, Bob got drunk one evening and stuck a broom in the campfire. He swung the broom torch around, sayin' he was gonna burn the Kaiser, but he accidentally caught a bystander woman's hair on fire instead. She wasn't hurt, just got her hair burned, but she took Bob to court and told Judge Metz what happened. The judge thought about it for a little while and said, "You're lucky. There are thousands of boys lyin' dead overseas, and you're complaining about a little scorched hair. Case dismissed."

Bob had a lively life although he smoked Bull Durham cigarettes, roll-your-own, of course. He had a moustache with a hole in one side that was a perfect fit for that cigarette. It made a pretty funny sight if he didn't have a cigarette. Bob could always make a person laugh.

Like I told you, Annie, my grandmother, told me and my mom most of these stories; I hadn't been born yet. Annie, my grandmother, was raised on the Fenton place. Annie was probably about 20 years old when she met the love of her life, Frank Lundie, and they married. The union took place in Idaho. After they married, they came back to Wyoming and settled down in Meeteetse, where he became the sheriff. He was a man of very few words, but when he spoke, his words were straight and true. Annie was a wonderful cook; I can still taste it. She also loved her canary birds and geraniums that she collected while traveling with Frank. She met different ladies that gave her the birds and geranium slips. Frank and Annie had one child, my mother Florence. After raising Florence, my grandparents traveled a lot and always looked forward to the fall season when they'd get ready to move on. Granddad liked the gold mines and gold fields, where he worked in many states during the winter.

On one trip, my grandparents were coming back from the gold fields to Wyoming. Outside Denver, they started to cross railroad tracks, and a train hit the car. The whole miracle was that neither of my grandparents was killed; they never lost their birds or dogs; and grandma saved all her geraniums. The railroad folks took them to the hospital to check them over and found they were fine. The railroad treated them wonderful, bought them a brand new car, paid their hospital bills, and the railroad even took care of the geraniums, birds, and dogs.

In the summer, my granddad was superintendent of the Pilot Ranches for Henry Coe, owner. Henry Sales was my granddad's boss and ran the Pilot Ranch year-round. The Two Dot was run by E. V. Robeson, who was the superintendent for all of Coe's holdings in the United States since Mr. Coe lived in England. My uncle, Harry Thayer, ran the Pitch Fork Ranch, which was also part of Coe's land.

All these ranches spread from prittin' near Meeteetse all the way to Cody, about 30 miles.

One summer when I was stayin' with grandma and grandpa on the Pilot Ranch, Mr. Coe showed up in a fancy car, which was the first damn car I'd ever seen. It was driven by a black man and I'd never seen one of them either. My grandparents were supposed to go on vacation per Mr. Coe's request and the driver would be the cook while they were gone. But Annie wouldn't allow a "nigger" in her kitchen and she told Frank that they would be leavin' for good if that black man came into her house. Mr. Coe wanted to talk about this, but Annie refused. Finally, after some persuasion, Mr. Coe talked to Annie about the situation. The only reason she agreed with Mr. Coe was that she found out that Grannie Specks and Mr. Coe were from the same town in England, Piccadilly.

The reason Mr. Coe showed up at the Pilot Ranch was 'cuz he was goin' on a bear hunt and the ranch was gonna be his headquarters. Mr. Coe brought five little white dogs with him in the car. He said they were bear dogs and gave me $5 *not* to play with 'em 'cuz they were huntin' dogs. That was the first money I ever earned. I was about seven or eight years old.

Mr. Coe wanted to go huntin' and fishin' 'cuz the Greybull River in those days had lots of white fish and trout. My granddad took Mr. Coe and me to a bridge over the river and tied me to it so I wouldn't fall in and drown. My granddad said to Mr. Coe, "You're next," and tied Mr. Coe up too.

Mr. Coe then told me, "I have a wonderful ranch foreman and I'm glad he tied us up 'cuz that river makes me dizzy."

In them days, Mr. Coe knew a lot of important people. Charlie Beldon was a famous photographer who associated with Mr. Coe and the other ranch superintendents like my uncle, Harry Thayer. Mr. Beldon made a million dollars on one photograph of a horned Hereford bull bellowin' on a mountain trail up at the head of the Greybull River.

Mr. Coe had a string of race horses that he sent from England to the Two Dot Ranch to get them fit at a higher elevation so he could take them to the Kentucky Derby at Churchill Downs and other big-payin' races. When we lived on the Thayer homestead, the Two Dot Ranch was pretty close, and that's where Bill Ur, Mr. Coe's head jockey and manager of the race horses, worked. Ur was an uncommon name, but he was English like my ancestors and Mr. Coe. We always called him Mr. Ur 'cuz we were learnt to call him that. Just like we were learnt to call black folks "niggers" back in those days, it was all we knew. Being kids, we didn't know it was so wrong. It's what we heard growin' up and sometimes I still say it 'cuz I didn't know it was wrong.

My granddad, Frank Lundie, came from Canada where his family was at the time. Remember, in those days, Canada belonged to England, so most Canadians were really English. Anyway, as a young man, Granddad worked the gold fields and mines in Canada. Then he migrated to the United States, married my grandma, and settled in Meeteetse in the summer but mined for gold in Arizona, Nevada, and California in the winter. Later, Granddad became a U.S. Marshall for the Northern Wyoming Territory. When Wyoming became a state on May 24, 1890, politics stepped into the picture, and many U.S. Marshalls were replaced with state police and county sheriffs. Since they did away with all of the U.S. Marshalls, my granddad then became sheriff of Meeteetse around the turn of the century. He had many adventures as a sheriff that my grandma told me about.

Accordin' to my granddad, the word Meeteetse is an Indian word. It seems that Granddad, a group of men, and an outside surveyor were locatin' a township which at the time was 36 sections of land—a mighty big area. Some folks wanted the town outside of the township, so the men decided to talk to the old Indian who was camped on the Greybull River where the town of Meeteetse now stands. The Indian would always greet the men by sayin' somethin' like "Meeteetse," which they thought meant, "Come to my teepee." The men didn't know what language the Indian spoke, but they named the town the best they could. That's what Granddad told me and who knows what tribe of Indians had such a word. I don't know if it was Shoshone or Crow or what. I just know the story.

Now days, lots of animal lovers like to go to Meeteetse, Wyoming, 'cuz of a little critter named the black-footed ferret. People thought the ferret was extinct until they found some in the Meeteetse area, which put the town on the map again in the 1970s or so. There are two museums in Meeteetse these days, and they both have black-footed ferret exhibits, I think. I know one has a big exhibit about that little critter.

Another little critter was a peg-legged guy everyone called Peggy Nolan 'cuz he had only one leg. He was quite a rebel since he drank whiskey and fought a lot with his peg leg as his main weapon. My granddad had been informed that Peggy would pick a fight with someone and fake an injury to his one good leg. Then Peggy would beat the hell out of whoever was feelin' sorry for him with his wooden leg.

Well, one night, my granddad was called to the saloon 'cuz there was a ruckus that Peggy Nolan was creatin'. My granddad deputized two bystanders to help him go arrest Peggy. Granddad showed up at the saloon, and sure enough, Peggy was on the floor, drunk. Granddad told him to get up and behave himself 'cuz he was fakin' an injury.

Peggy said, "No tin horn is gonna tell me what to do."

Granddad took his belly club and tapped Peggy on the head, tellin' the deputies, "Take him and his peg leg to jail and tie him up."

The Meeteetse jail was made out of slabs of wood and didn't have cells at that time. So to keep a criminal a prisoner, Granddad had to tie him up with rope and pegs in the ground. Granddad said he didn't have enough sense to search the criminals who could have just taken a pocketknife and cut themselves loose. Granddad would have been real upset if anyone ever tried to escape. In them days, the outhouses had more security than the jail.

Another time, a man passed on, and since there was no mortuaries, the man was laid out in a shed. The custom of the time was to have someone sit up with the dead person during the day and night. My granddad looked around to find someone to watch the corpse, and he found a man who liked his whiskey, but he was the only man

Granddad could find. So the man told my granddad, "If you buy me a pint of whiskey, I will sit up with him."

Later, my granddad went to check on him and the corpse. When Granddad got there, he saw the live man was still sittin' in the corner "fogged out." The corpse was laid on the floor with his pants' pockets turned the wrong side out. The live man had gotten drunk on the pint of whiskey and searched the corpse for a match to light his pipe. Whiskey can be dangerous, even to a corpse!

Once, my granddad was told there was a horse thief around Meeteetse. Horse thieves in them days were hanged. In a few days, a man rode in and told my granddad that he knew who stole the horse. My granddad picked out two men to investigate. Sure enough, they found a Mexican sheepherder ridin' the stolen horse.

The lawmen decided they had to give the Mexican a fair hearin' before they hung him. Granddad rounded up three other men, which made a six-man "jury" as required to hang a man legally in them days. The jury decided they should have a gallon of whiskey and talk the situation over. They all got pie-eyed, includin' the Mexican sheepherder who couldn't speak English.

My granddad said, "The drunker we got, the more innocent the Mexican looked."

They took the Mexican to the Meeteetse jail and tied him up with a rope for a few days. My granddad finally got notice that another guy had stolen the Meeteetse horse, then rode out and found the Mexican sheepherder. The guy then stole the sheepherder's horse and left him the Meeteetse horse.

Granddad happily said, "Thank God we didn't hang an innocent man."

The real horse thief was probably hanged by the ones who found the sheepherder's horse. I don't know for sure, but that's how people took care of things back then.

My dad, George, had a Model T car that was brought into Cody, where there was no gas to buy for it, so they had to bring eight jars of gas into Cody too. That car was the first car in the town of Meeteetse. When he drove it from Cody, it took about eight hours 'cuz him and his friend, Willy, had to get the car out of lots of deep ruts in the road. Sometimes, they had to lift the whole car up and put it on solid ground, then go on until they hit another rut.

In Meeteetse, lots of buggies and horses were tied up to the hitchin' posts along the street. Since no one or no horse had ever heard or seen a car before, everything went haywire. The horses pulled back, broke their halters, their bridles, and ran away. Granddad said it was really a mess with horses runnin' here and there and buggies turned over in the street.

Granddad had to arrest my dad for causin' a mess in the middle of the street and kept him tied up for two days. My grandma had to feed the prisoners, so she saw who was in jail and why. My mother thought it was awful that a man would tie up his own son-in-law and put him in jail. Later, Mama said that she wished her dad had kept her husband there for a much longer time.

One night, a man knocked at my grandparents' door and told my granddad there had been a murder at Arland, Wyoming. Arland was a very small town with only two or three houses and a roadhouse about five or six miles west of Meeteetse, up the Meeteetse Creek Road. Arland got its name from the man that helped build the roadhouse which was a really wild place back in the early days.

My granddad had to investigate the reported murder, so he deputized a man to go with him and they headed up to Arland. Sure enough, there had been a murder, but no corpse could be found.

The operator of the roadhouse, Pete Peron, was asked where the corpse was.

Pete said, "He's out behind the roadhouse gettin' cooled off."

Well, my granddad asked, "What's the water on the floor?"

Pete said, "You don't expect us to play cards with blood and brains all over the floor, do ya?"

Then my granddad said, "Who killed him?"

Pete said, "I did."

Two or three other men confirmed that Pete had shot the man.

"Why?" Granddad asked.

"'Cuz I accused him of cheatin'. So he went for his gun, and I blew his brains out."

The other men verified Pete's statement. End of case—that's all my granddad needed to determine self-defense.

The next day, Granddad sent a buggy up to Arland to pick up the corpse. It was buried in the Meeteetse Creek Cemetery where most of my dad's relatives, including him, are also buried. Alice and Will Thayer, my paternal grandparents, and Grannie Specks, along with several other aunts and uncles, are buried there too. A fast lady from Meeteetse is also buried up there.

Rosa, the fast lady, was called Rose by my granddad. Other people called her a whore. She had a packhorse and a saddle horse that she travelled with from sheep camp to cow camp. She travelled all over at the request of the sheepherders and cowboys who would tell their bosses that they wanted Rose to visit. She would go there for a day or two before going to the next camp to take care of other cowboys and sheepherders. The sheepherders and cowboys didn't keep money with them, so the bosses had to advance them money so Rosa could get paid for her services at their camps. My granddad said Rosa always had plenty of business.

Grandma and four or five other ladies were the only women in Meeteetse at the time, and every one of them hated Rosa or any woman pullin' that kind of stuff. Sometimes, sheepherders or cowboys would come to Meeteetse, get drunk, and want to see Rosa. But Rosa was often out on the trail between other camps doin' her job.

One day, a guy showed up in Meeteetse who said that he had been to see Rosa who was really sick and had sent him to find my granddad. Granddad tried to get in touch with the local medicine man since there were no doctors around. The medicine man was not an Indian but someone who went around helpin' sick people. Since Rosa had no family or friends except her customers, granddad had to go see Rosa 'cuz the medicine man could not be found. When granddad got there, Rosa knew the end was near and told him that she wanted to be buried at the Meeteetse Creek Cemetery along with her fine jewelry. Granddad made sure her final wishes were carried out, jewelry and all.

During the flu epidemic of 1917–18 during WWI, many people died across the world and in Meeteetse. Grandma, my mom and everyone were under quarantine. The only way families kept in touch with one another was by wavin' dishcloths from the windows at each others' houses to tell them everything was OK. No one could go outside; no one wanted to. Luckily, no one in my family died.

I think the Asafetida worked, but it was really a stinkin' SOB. If you ever smelled of it, it smelled like rotten cat manure. Every one of us kids had to wear it, and so did the parents and grandparents. A cheesecloth ball about one inch around held the stinkin' stuff on a string that we hung around our necks. It used to be sold at drugstores. Once, I asked a pharmacist in Lander if he had any.

He said, "If we still used Asafetida, we wouldn't have any drugstores."

He was right too. That stuff was powerful. I can still smell it although I haven't been around it in over 80 years. They used it for diphtheria, small pox, measles, whoppin' cough, and everything 'cuz we didn't have drugs like today. The only one thing they couldn't use it for was tick fever, which killed a lot of people too.

One day, my granddad met Pete Peron in Meeteetse. Now, my granddad and Pete were both from Canada, but my granddad rode a saddle horse to Wyoming 'cuz there were no trains or cars. Pete Peron was forced to leave Canada. He told my granddad why he came to Meeteetse.

There was a flood at Lethbridge, Canada, that killed a whole bunch of people. Pete was an orphan about seventeen years old then. He went around and stole the jewelry, watches, or anything of value off the dead corpses that were killed by the flood. The "red coats," the British police in Canada, got wind of him robbin' the dead, so Pete left Canada in a hurry and went over into Montana.

While Pete was playin' cards in Montana, a U.S. Army officer tapped Pete on the shoulder and said, "Are you Pete Peron?"

Pete said that before he could answer, the officer continued, "I know damn well you are Pete Peron. So I'm givin' you two choices. One, go back to Canada, or two, join the U.S. Army to fight in the Spanish-American War. What will it be?"

Well, Pete said he didn't have to think very long. He knew if he went back to Canada, they'd hang him, so he took the army.

Now, let me tell you about my parents, George and Florence Thayer, who got married in Meeteetse, Wyoming, around the turn of the century. I know some information about my Thayer bloodline thanks to a man named Robert Bennion. Mr. Bennion came to my house in Cody in 2007 and hand-delivered to my wife some family trees that he had researched. Those papers dated clear back to my Thayer great-great-grandparents. According to those papers, my great-great-grandpa was Leonard Thayer, who was married to Elizabeth Fowler. They were William Thayer's parents. My great-great grandparents from the women's side were named John Cromer and Christina Warner. We can guess that my great-great grandparents were born in the late 1700s. From this information, my family is related to people named Cromer, Fowler, and Warner.

The papers also have pictures of these people, including my great-grandpa who was named Nelson Thayer and was born on February 22, 1818. Nelson married Mary Lucy Cromer on June 15, 1847, in White County, Indiana. Lucy was born near Buffalo, New York, on February 15, 1831. Their pictures were taken when they're pretty old, maybe in the late 1800s too. Nelson died on March 22, 1902, at the age of 74 which is pretty amazing since most people didn't live that long back then. Mary died on January 17, 1901 and is buried in Ponca City, Oklahoma, where Nelson is too. Nelson and Mary had fourteen children, but only eleven lived to adulthood. One of them was my paternal grandpa, William Thayer.

I'm not sure how any of the Thayers were related to a man who became Governor of Oregon, but it was way back a long time ago, maybe when it first became a state. The man's name was W. W. Thayer. I learned this was from another man who came to my door, this time in St. Helens, Oregon. He was tryin' to sell me Fuller brushes. He told me that he was a Thayer too and that we were related. Then he explained to me that his family was the family that started Thayer Junction, Wyoming. The nearest I could understand from the man since he was pretty old back then was that my granddad, William, had a brother named Wilson. I'm not sure, but maybe Wilson and his family started Thayer Junction, Wyoming.

William Thayer, my grandpa, was born on January 2, 1849, in Dallas County, Iowa. William married Alice McDonough on October 13, 1872. Alice was born on January 3, 1854, in Le Seaur, Minnesota. Their marriage and the McDonough name was why Mr. Bennion came to my house and how one of my uncles was named McDonough Thayer. McDonough Thayer married Edith Amelia Todd in Billings, Montana, on August 13, 1906. Their firstborn child was named Hazel Thayer who was born on June 13, 1907, in Fenton, Wyoming. Hazel married Raymond Bennion on July 2, 1925, in Cody, Wyoming. Their son was named Robert. He's the man who showed up at my door in Cody; he's my relative, but I had never met him or heard of him.

My great-aunt, Martha Thayer, was a sister to my grandpa, William Thayer. Martha married a man named John McCoy. John's father developed the Blue Lake Bean that grew on poles and was a bush bean too—a real McCoy. John had a contract with the U.S. Military durin' WWII to grow beans for the armed forces. He had hundreds of acres in Salem, Oregon, planted in Blue Lake beans and employed two hundred pickers to get them out of the field. They were a really good bean and sure fed a lot of men, so the real McCoys are my relatives too.

Even though I had these papers with Thayer information all the way back to 1818, my friend, Karen King, taught me how to read 'em in 2015. We traced my lineage on the Thayer side back five generations from me. There's more information I can add to those papers about what I know that maybe Mr. Bennion didn't know. Another interesting thing about these papers is the pictures. I can't imagine how they afforded to take those Thayer pictures since I don't have many of my Fenton family. Karen told me the pictures probably came off the Internet, which I don't understand. The only net I know about is somethin' you fish with. I guess you can find lots of stuff on the Internet that other people have found. Karen says the Internet is like the biggest library in the whole world. It must be. To have those old pictures is really somethin'.

My dad told me about old pictures and how they were made. The old photograph equipment was a tripod and a camera machine; I don't know what you call them, but the photographer threw a black cloth over his head and took a picture. I've got some really old pictures of my dad's freight business with five teams, a total of ten horses. I don't know who or how they took those pictures, but they're from the late 1800s. I got them enlarged at Francis Gilbert's photo shop in Portland, Oregon, around the 1960s and still have them right now. I have an old picture of me, just a snot-nosed kid too. I'm ridin' an orphaned ram that we used to spoil and my sister, Annie, and brother, Sid, are standin' near.

My dad's folks homesteaded just north of Meeteetse where they raised their fairly large family. One of my dad's brothers, Harry, ran the Pitch Fork Ranch, and their dad ran the Meeteetse Thayer place. My Thayer grandparents had two sections of land at Meeteetse, and they set seven acres aside for the Meeteetse Creek Cemetery where a lot of my ancestors, including my dad and Grannie Specks, are buried. My Thayer great-grandparents operated a tradin' post east of Rock Springs called Thayer Junction. They also traded fat cattle and horses for poor cattle and horses to the pioneers who were continuin' their journeys to the west coast. These Thayers were driven out of business when the railroad came through southern Wyoming. They moved on to Oregon where one of my relatives became governor.

My mother and dad met in Meeteetse, got acquainted, and got married there since my mom grew up in Fenton about sixteen miles northeast of Meeteetse. George and Florence started their new life together by runnin' wild horses that they found just anywhere across the wide-open spaces. Back then, they were called "slicks" or horses without a brand. My folks would sell the slicks or keep them for their own.

Years after their wild horse spree, they left their cabin at Old Arland and the signal post that people used to communicate with. If folks had trouble, they'd run a flag up the pole that could be seen from a distance and let one another know they needed help. There was no telephones, electricity, or indoor plumbin' in those days, but we made it just fine. We were used to livin' that way. Anyway, my folks moved back to Meeteetse where over a few years, my mom had my six older brothers and sisters. Jacky was stillborn, George "Bugs", Charlie, Mary, Sid, and Myrtle were the older siblings.

Mama taught the oldest kids 'cuz there wasn't a school in Meeteetse at the time. The closest school was in Long Hollow prittin' near six miles west of Meeteetse up Meeteetse Creek, which didn't have a road, just a trail. My grandma would take care of the littler kids while Mama filled in at Long Hollow School and taught the older kids sometimes if the teacher was gone. Eventually, Mama became the only teacher at Long Hollow.

There was the Simpson kids that went there too, including Milward, who later became the father of Al Simpson, a U.S. senator from Wyoming, and Pete Simpson, a candidate for Wyoming Governor. Milward's brother, Bill, also went to Long Hollow School. Dusty and Adolph Keiler, who were part Shoshone Indian, went there too. The Webster kids, Slack kids, and the four older Thayer kids (Bugs, Mary, Charlie, and Sid) went to school there with about 15-20 kids total. But, I never went to Long Hollow School.

Durin' that time, my dad worked at various ranches. When another job came up, they moved back to Old Arland to take care of a man named Pete Peron. He was an old Spanish-American War veteran that my granddad had met previously. My folks' new job was to live in Pete's house with the six older children and take care of Pete. Every day, Pete let them know he was the boss. Anything that came up that Pete didn't like, he went for his shotgun.

I was born in Pete Peron's place in Old Arland. I got my first name after my granddad, Frank Lundie, and my middle name from Pete Peron. Mom said they figured that by namin' me Pete, old Pete would settle down, but it turned out to be the worst thing. I became his "Little Man," and whenever I bawled, he was sure Mama was mistreatin' me, and Pete would threaten her with his shotgun.

My folks told me that one day, my dad was comin' home from work, and he met Mr. Peron walkin' down the trail. He asked him where he was goin'. Mr. Peron said, "I'm goin' to hell. Would you like to come along?"

He had his cane in one hand and his shotgun under the other arm. Pete said a damned gypsy woman had robbed him and he was gonna blow her brains out for stealin' a $20 gold piece from him.

Dad had just ridden by the gypsy camp, so he turned his horse around and went back to the camp to talk to them. The gypsy lady said she didn't rob Pete.

Dad told her, "You better be sure 'cuz he's comin' down the trail right now with his shotgun."

It was late in the day, and the gypsies didn't have time to move their camp. Yep, the gypsy lady went into her tent and came back out with a $20 gold piece and said, "I must have misplaced it in my purse."

Dad went back up the trail while Pete was comin' closer. Finally, Dad got Pete on his saddle horse along with his shotgun and cane and led the horse back home. When they got home, Dad put the $20 gold piece on Pete's nightstand tellin' old Pete he must have overlooked it earlier. That made Pete happy.

Pete always liked my dad and brothers, but he really didn't like Mama much or any other woman since Pete never did marry. Later that night, Dad rode into Meeteetse and told my granddad what took place. Granddad went to the gypsy camp and told them to move on and, yep, they did even in the dark of night.

Back at Old Arland, something was killin' Pete's pigeons. He said it was a wildcat. One day, my folks were waitin' for Pete to come to dinner and they heard a shot. They went out to see what took place and there was Pete cryin' real hard holdin' his pet cat, not a wildcat. Pete had killed his own tomcat by mistake.

Right then was when my dad loaded all of Pete's shotgun shells with blanks. Every time he shot a blank, Pete would say, "I think

I'm losin' my eyesight." He didn't know the difference since he was really old by then.

Once, Pete was takin' a bath with my dad helpin' him into the washtub on the porch when Mama heard a loud ruckus outside. Dad had just stepped off the porch for a minute or two when Pete tried to get out of the tub and it tipped over on him. He was lyin' facedown, squealin', and swearin'. Pete was caught under the tub and Dad had to free him. Over the next day or two, Pete accused Mama of tippin' the tub over on him.

Later, Dad went to the Meeteetse Post Office and saw a sign that asked people to report any old veterans 'cuz they wanted to help those who fought in the Spanish-American War. Dad told the postmaster about Pete. The postmaster, in turn, told some folks in Sheridan about Pete. The Sheridan folks told the postmaster who told my dad that they were comin' to interview Pete and my folks.

That's why Pete was takin' a bath. Mama said he really hated water maybe 'cuz of the Lethbridge flood decades earlier. Back in those days, there were no rest homes like today, but in Sheridan, they had just built a veterans home.

A day or two after his bath, there was a buggy that showed up at Old Arland. The driver and another man wanted to talk to Mr. Peron. After a few minutes of talkin' with Pete, they decided to take him to the Sheridan Veterans Home that day. Mama said she was sad and happy to see Pete go. Sad 'cuz he kept sayin', "Help me," and happy 'cuz Mama and Dad didn't have to worry anymore about Pete killin' anyone else, especially their kids.

Pete is buried in the Veterans Cemetery in Sheridan, Wyoming. My mom and dad told us in later years about Pete since I was just his "Little Man," as he always called me.

My folks lived at the Goodykoonts' Ranch outside Meeteetse where that family had been ranchers and operators of a freight business for some years. That's how my dad got into the freight business. Dad went to the Meeteetse Bank and Mr. Graham at the bank told him the Goodykoonts' place and freight business was for sale. Mr. Graham said that the bank would finance the purchase of the ranch and the freight line if Dad wanted it. Well, that's what happened. Prittin' near all seven of my younger brothers and sisters (Scottie, Nellie, Alberta, Pansy, Annie, Carl) were born in Sunshine Basin on the Goodykoonts' place. I was the only one born in Old Arland and Jerry was the only one born in Cody.

Dad said they had to work really hard in that freight business. Gettin' up early, feedin' all the livestock, harnessin' the teams, eatin' their breakfast, and then hittin' the trails took probably two or three hours each day before the sun came up. For the freight business, Dad hauled a trap wagon that carried the horses' food, extra groceries for the people, tents and supplies for bad weather, and extra supplies in case a horse threw a shoe or a wagon or harness needed to be repaired.

Parts of the harness included a tug which was made of leather and attached to the hames, the two curved wooden parts of the harness. The hame was then attached to the collar that went around the horse's neck. The double tree is part of the wagon and harness. Double tree is for two horses and a single tree is for one horse. The trees hook the horses to the wagon so it can be pulled. The tugs hook into the trees. Any of these parts or other wagon parts could break, so spare parts were always taken along in the trap wagon. I was just a little snot-nosed kid so I didn't have anything to do with haulin' freight but I sure learned about horses and all the tack to keep wagons movin'.

Farm equipment like hay stackers, mowin' machines, buck or hay rakes, were moved between Cody and Meeteetse. You name it, Dad hauled it. Dad would sometimes haul us kids back to the Fenton place to visit with Uncle Bob's family or to Meeteetse to see our grandparents. Granddad told me about the freight business before the railroads came. Dependin' on the size of the haul, they'd use two to eight teams of horses. During the spring of the year, they hauled a lot of wool, which is plumb heavy. Ten sacks of wool were sometimes hauled per wagon. Each sack had about five hundred pounds of wool in it so ten sacks of wool weighed about five thousand pounds. That's why they needed sixteen head of horses to carry the freight over all those hills between Meeteetse and Cody.

Roads really didn't exist back then. Wagon trails was all there was. Haulin' freight over these trails meant you had to have a lot of horsepower. The only thing for transportation in those days was horsepower, the real thing, powered by hay not gasoline.

My dad went out of the freight business after a few years 'cuz the railroad came to Cody, and it was really hard work. He started delivering the U.S. mail from Meeteetse to Cody which he did for several years. Times were gettin' better, and more cars were around, but my dad delivered mail by horse and buggy in that part of Wyoming for many years. Eventually, Dad bought a truck called a White that he traded the horse and buggy for. The truck was faster than a horse and buggy, but the work wasn't that much easier 'cuz there were still dirt roads and a lot of breakdowns.

During the time Dad was drivin' the mail, he and Mama took up a homestead on Sage Creek between Wiley, Wyoming, and the Two Dot Ranch, about eighteen miles north of Meeteetse. All that Wiley had was a reservoir and a couple of houses. Those 640 acres became known as the Thayer Homestead where they raised cattle, horses, sheep and rattle snakes—boy, we had a lot of 'em. Sage hens, antelope, deer, and pheasant were plentiful there too. Every once in a while, elk would come down Sage Creek. You name it, we had it there. We moved to the Thayer Homestead after we left the Goodykoonts' place.

I went to first grade at the Sage Creek School and by fourth grade I was in school in Cody. Yep, we moved again when I was about nine years old. We had to leave the homestead all 'cuz of education. The Thayer, Feely, and Avery kids were the only ones going to Sage Creek School, a little one-room building at the time. The county made us move to Cody 'cuz the public schools there had started, and they didn't cost as much to run as a country school. The small schools had to consolidate with the big schools across Park County and the whole state of Wyoming 'cuz of money.

Mama had taught her own kids at the Goodykoonts' place and at Sage Creek with the Avery and Feely kids. Now, remember, she taught at Long Hollow, which was about five miles northwest of

Meeteetse, up Meeteetse Creek. And that didn't cost the state or county anything for a lot of years.

Anyway, on Sage Creek is where the Avery kids lived. They were named Maude and Osee, and their mother was also named Maude. One day, our school went on a picnic and Osee took my brand new shoe and threw it in Sage Creek, which was runnin' pretty big 'cuz it was springtime. Hell's fire, a pair of shoes in those days cost 75¢ and no one wanted to throw that kind of money away. Young Maude and all the school kids looked for that shoe for a long time. Then the parents came and everyone looked for that shoe too. Maude was ready to kill her daughter for doin' somethin' so wasteful. To this day, no one has found that shoe.

Every kid had to do chores for the school. Some of us cut wood, stacked wood, hauled ashes or more wood that kept the school warm. Kids kept the school clean too. My job was to carry in the kindlin' during the wintertime. There was a real tall school master at the time that made sure all the kids did their chores. I don't remember anyone gettin' in big trouble in those days 'cuz we listened to what the adults told us and we did it with no sass. We knew if we got in trouble at school, we'd be in bigger trouble at home.

Mama or Bugs would take care of that. Mama never touched us boys, that was Bugs' job to correct us. Mama took care of the girls. When Carl was little, Bugs told him to lie across his lap like he was gonna spank him. Carl did what he was told. Bugs never spanked him, just clapped his hands together, but Carl cried anyway. We all laughed, as long as it didn't happen to us.

My parents had a total of fourteen children. Jacky died as a baby, and I was the seventh in line. My youngest brother, Jerry, was the only one my mother had a doctor for. She always used a midwife with the other kids' births. Jerry was born at our home in Cody since there was no hospital back then. Jerry caught pneumonia as a newborn, and Dr. Llewelyn told Mama that Jerry wasn't gonna make it. He said he'd be back in the mornin' with a death certificate and he left some medicine to give Jerry. My sister, Mary, took care of Jerry that night 'cuz Mama was played out from the birthin'. Mary ran out of the medicine and decided to give Jerry a couple of drops of whiskey every once and a while like Mama used to do instead.

This is the God's truth. Jerry started to get better, and when Dr. Llewelyn showed up the next mornin', Mama went to the door. Dr. Llewlyn tried to hand Mama an envelope with the death certificate in it.

Mama said, "I don't need it. Jerry is alive."

Dr. Llewlyn came in and gave Jerry a checkup since they didn't have equipment other than their eyes and hands to use on sick babies.

He asked Ma and Mary, "What did you do for this baby when you ran out of the medicine I gave you?"

They told him they gave Jerry just a little whiskey.

Dr. Llewelyn said, "Keep doin' whatever you're doin'. He's gettin' along fine."

Ma thought so much of Dr. Llewelyn that she gave Jerry the middle name of Llewelyn.

Most of us Thayer kids, includin' Jerry, went to school in Cody. We lived on the Walls' place, a ranch about a half mile east of downtown Cody on the hill where Albertson's Grocery Store is now. We rode our horses to school in bad weather or took the buggy. There was a barn at the school where the horses would be tied until we rode 'em home after school. Sometimes we walked to school if the weather was nice. I went through the eighth grade at Cody, which was the legal age to leave school back then, and that was exactly when I left formal schoolin', but I sure kept learnin'.

I learnt some things I didn't really want to know either. Our teachers always told us to study hard 'cuz we would never go to college. That's the God's truth. The teachers didn't expect much of us country kids. I sure learnt more in my life bein' on my own than I ever learnt in school. The military and all the jobs I held taught me a lot.

I learnt a lot when I was about five or six from Charlie Phillips, my brother-in-law, who married Myrtle, when he'd take me fishin'. Charlie taught me to fish and to hunt with a .22 rifle for cottontails. Once, we were fishin' on the Stinkin' Water, named that 'cuz there are a lot of sulfur springs along its banks. Today's high-falutin' Cody folks call the Stinkin' Water the Shoshone River now.

We had a favorite fishin' hole on that river, whatever you want to call it. At that time, Texaco Refinery drained their used oil right into the river, and when it hit the cold water it caused a waxy scum on top. We'd cast our lines by the scum and those fish would bite like crazy 'cuz under the scum, it was nice and shady for them. The fish would go under the oil slick and really strike hard at our angle worms or grasshoppers or whatever we could find for bait. We never had fancy flies or lures. For a fishin' pole, all we used was a willow branch, some fishin' line and a hook.

One day, I snagged a great big fish. He must have been prittin' near two feet long. I got him on the line, but he broke loose. I was so mad I went chargin' after him and fell on the slippery rocks by the river tryin' to catch him again. By gum, if that same fish didn't go and bite Charlie's line. That big ol' fish broke Charlie's line too and Charlie let out some cuss words. We never did land that fish, but that night, I dreamed about that big trout. I still think about that fish, but it kinda broke my spirit for fishin'. I never cared much for fishin' after that.

Charlie and I used to hunt for cottontail rabbits with a single shot .22 rifle. There was thousands of rabbits all over. We'd go early in the mornin' when the rabbits were sittin' by the rocks, sunnin' themselves. That's the best time to hunt rabbits. Believe this or not, havin' rabbit and fish to eat in our home were real delicacies. We always had plenty of beef, pork, and mutton 'cuz we raised it ourselves. We never knew about salmon, crabs, or other seafood until they started to sell 'em in the stores.

Now, when I was a kid and folks would cut the hay, sometimes, a mother sage chicken would be sittin' in the hayfield and she'd fly away from the nest to never return. That meant the eggs wouldn't hatch. So we'd take the eggs and set them under a chicken until they hatched. The settin' hen would raise them up until the baby sage chickens were ready to be on their own. All we were tryin' to do was let the little birds be born and have a life. We never could make money off 'em.

At Christmas time, Mama would fix a big meal for the old men who lived on the Poor Farm outside Cody. In those days, there were no nursin' homes, so they'd take the old men and put them in one bunch and the old ladies in another. They'd split a piece of land so the women were separate from the men. The old men would take care of all the gardens and take the produce to the old ladies who would can it and put it up. That's the way they stayed alive—sharin' work and food. That's the way we stayed alive too, by God.

One of my younger brothers, Carl, and I barely stayed alive when we went out ridin' bareback and barefooted to a place called Horse Center. It was called that 'cuz there was always a lot of wild horses there. I was told there once was an old volcano at that spot. It was a great big valley with all kinds of hills around it, and the horses really liked it there.

Once when we crossed Horse Center, we ran into a big rattle snake. I jumped off my horse and killed it with a rock. We decided we'd skin it. Only thing was, we were tryin' to skin the snake while we were sittin' horseback. Carl was holdin' one end of the snake and I was skinnin' the other. All at once, the snake's rattle went off and we went airborne, both of us. Our horses bucked our asses right off when they heard those rattles. They took off for home, leavin' us afoot to walk all the way back to the Walls' place, about eight or nine miles, and we couldn't walk barefoot on the road 'cuz it was all gravel.

Mama got nervous when the horses came home without us kids. She told a delivery boy called Hanson who was drivin' a truck to look for her sons if he delivered the way of Horse Center. If he saw us, Mama told him *not* to give us a ride, but to let us walk home.

When that SOB drove by us, Carl shook his fists 'cuz he didn't pick us up. Walkin' through the sagebrush and prickly pears sure made our feet sore, but we made it home somehow.

Mama, bless her heart, said, "Maybe next time, you'll do as I tell you since I told you not to go very far."

Carl and I both spent the next few hours soakin' our feet in the washtub filled with Epsom salts. That really felt good. Sure felt lots better than what we'd been walkin' through to get back home.

When I went to junior high school in Cody, I played football. One incident I want to tell about was playin' against Powell. Since we didn't have any buses, folks just took us in their cars or trucks to Powell for the game. I always rode with someone else since we didn't have a car then. When we got to Powell, all we had was our boots, cowboy hats, and regular clothes. Powell's team marched out with helmets, cleats, and everything else that was available to play the game. We had nothin'.

I remember I was playin' right guard and there was a big, tall Mexican kid on the Powell team. Me, bein' a bonehead, thought I could out-bunt his helmet with my bare head. Well, that about murdered me. Mr. Switzer, our coach, called me to the sidelines. I better not tell you, but I will, he called me an asshole and told me that I couldn't out-bunt anyone with a helmet.

He let me rest a little while 'cuz I had a deep cut on my head. Then he said, "Pete, I'm gonna tell you how to take care of that guy. Go back out there, and when he tries to bunt you, since he's so tall, put your head down and come back up from underneath and hit him hard."

Well, I broke his nose and knocked him silly. The refs called both of us out of the game.

One of the gals who helped the team with first aid and watched the game called me a brute 'cuz I broke her boyfriend's nose. Lo and behold, she married that Mexican. Later, they got a divorce 'cuz all the Mexican's family would only speak Spanish and she didn't. She told my sister that the Mexican family would look at her and then laugh 'cuz she didn't know what they were sayin'.

About 85 years after that game against Powell, I was waitin' to get a prescription filled at the pharmacy in Cody. I had to be outside 'cuz I can't stand the smell of a drugstore even to this day. Asafetida sure smells for a long time. Anyway, I was standin' on the sidewalk when

I glanced over and saw a policeman and another man talkin'. The man turned around and walked right toward me, doublin' up his fists.

He asked, "Are you Pete Thayer?"

I told him, "I was when I got up this morning."

He then said, "I've been waitin' a long time for this. You disfigured my brother's face by breakin' his nose at that Powell football game."

Then the old fart took a swing at me. Since I'd seen his fists, I was ready and just stepped aside. Bam! He hit the light post we were standin' by real hard. The policeman came runnin' over and took both of us to the Justice of the Peace. The Justice of the Peace told the policeman to take the man to the hospital and have his hand looked at.

The policeman told the man, "Go sober up. You're too old to be hittin' light posts."

We were both over 90 years old at the time, fightin' about something that happened when we were kids. Crazy old men, eh?

I didn't just play football in junior high; I also worked at various jobs. I worked on many ranches puttin' up hay, shearin' sheep, punchin' cows, herdin' sheep, packin' horses and trappin' coyotes, muskrats, and skunks. Shit, oh dear, muskrats were about 20¢ per hide. The most we ever got for skunks was $2. I guess they used skunk pee in women's perfume, so we had to save their pee too. For coyotes, we got about $2-$5 per hide dependin' on how good their fur was.

Right after I got out of school, I worked at Mammoth Hot Springs in Yellowstone Park. My job was water boy deliverin' drinkin' water to all the other crew members. They were puttin' in a new waterline and were diggin' through lots of mineral deposits. This work was all done with pick and shovels by hand. All the workers lived in the Mammoth Hotel since they gave us board and room. It was a WPA (Work Progress Administration) project that FDR put in place after he was elected president. The diggers were diggin' a ditch when the whole son-of-a-bitchin' bottom went straight down. I heard there were seven men who lost their lives that day. Later, a safety manager from Butte, Montana, showed up. He threw 50 feet of rope down that hole and still didn't reach bottom. I guess the men are still down there.

We had our share of family tragedy too. My brother Scottie was three years younger than me. He was born in 1918 with Nellie born in between us. One day, I went down to the barn to saddle up my horse to just go for a ride. Scottie came runnin' into the barn and spooked a mare that kicked him in the stomach. In them days, we never had a doctor close by or any way of gettin' X-rays like today, so we loaded him in the truck and headed to Billings to get him to a hospital. Scottie didn't make it past Powell. He died 'cuz the kick broke a main blood vessel to the stomach. A man in Powell had a sign out that said "Doctor." He had no education to be doctor, but pronounced Scottie dead. We turned around and took Scottie to Cody Mortuary and he's buried in the Cody Cemetery along with many of my other folks.

I was about sixteen or seventeen when I was walkin' down the street in Cody, and I heard a car horn honk. I went to the car where I saw a man that I worked for off and on. His name was Carl Thompson and asked me if I wanted to take a ride.

Well, I asked Carl, "To do what?"

Then he told me, "I need someone to take a string of horses that I sold in Cody to the buyer in Rock Springs."

I said, "Sure." Since I was out of work, I jumped at a chance to earn some money.

The next day, I started out at Wiley, where Mr. Thompson lived, and followed the Old Convict Road on a good saddle horse drivin' 36 horses and one mule by myself. It was called Old Convict Road or The Stock Trail 'cuz convicts built the road so wagons and stock could get across the hills. In fact, I've seen seven wooden crosses myself on the Old Convict Road 'cuz the convicts were worked to death to build that road. If they got sick, they died, and that was it. Anyway, I drove the horses to Two Dot Ranch and then to the head of Meeteetse Creek Rim. Then I went on down to the Big Rawhide, which is another creek that drains into Meeteetse Creek. I could go over the same route today if I had to, but I can't tell you the names without lookin' at the map. Here it is on this map. Right there's Wiley.

Mr. Thompson sent other people to meet me on the way and bring food and supplies when I met them at Big Rawhide. I went on to Francs Peak where Mr. Thompson had a band of sheep and some men. I stayed there one night and then I dropped down to the East Fork River at the base of Carter Mountain and made my way south toward Dubois about 96 miles. I made it that far in about a week. Mr. Thompson sent a supply man to the junction of the East Fork River and the Wind River where I stayed one night and he re-supplied me for the rest of the trip.

Since it was summertime, I crossed the Wind River near Dubois. I never went into the town of Dubois 'cuz it was still five or six miles west from where I crossed the Wind River. But the river was at pretty low water and I crossed without any problems, so we just continued on. If someone would furnish me a horse, I'd go over it again 'cuz it is such beautiful country.

You know, I don't think I ever crossed a fence that whole ride. Nope, there weren't any fences tearin' up the country back then. Today, I think you'd have to cut a lot of fences and cross lots of private property to get that far with a string of horses and one mule.

By the way, that mule was a lifesaver. She was called Jenny and Mr. Thompson said to stake her out at night so the horses would all stay with her. By gum, that's what they done. Every mornin', I'd wake up and there would be ole Jenny with all the horses right there too. She sure saved me a lot of work keepin' all those horses together on that trip.

I stayed low on the east side of the Wind River Mountains to Crowheart on the Wind River Indian Reservation. From Crowheart, I made it to the Red Canyon area outside of Lander and then on over South Pass toward Farson. I just kept headin' south and followin' the east side of the Wind River Mountains until I got to Farson.

When I got to Farson, I saw an old high-wheeled Dodge with a canvas top comin' up the road. The car didn't look like it had a driver. When it started past me, someone honked the horn and stopped.

I asked the tiny driver, "Can you tell me where the Bobalink Ranch is?"

Lo and behold, he said with a funny accent, "My-a name-a is-a Peter Bobalink-a."

To hear his voice and see such a short man with a huge moustache, I got plumb tickled.

He said, "Those are-a my a-horses."

I looked at the bill of sale that Mr. Thompson had sent with me and sure enough, Pete Bobalink was listed as the buyer of those horses.

Mr. Bobalink said in his funny accent, "You-a keep-a goin' a-down a-this a-road-a. I'll head a-down a-there a-too and-a be-a waitin'-a for-a you-a."

When I got there, Mr. Bobalink had me take my saddle and bridle off my horse and put them in his car. I put the horses and Jenny in a big pasture that Mr. Bobalink leased or owned—he had a hell of a lot of land.

Next thing, Pete said, "Get-a in-a, kid-a. We'll a-go a-home-a."

As we pulled up to the Bobalink place, I saw a girl about my age and her mother walkin' around in a big wooden tank.

I asked Mr. Bobalink, "What are they doin'?"

He said, "They're a-stompin' the grapes-a."

I asked him, "What's a grape-a?"

Mama never had us kids eat any grapes 'cuz they didn't grow around our part of Wyoming, and swear to God, I didn't know what he was talkin' about.

Mr. Bobalink then told me, "We make-a grapes-a into-a wine-a."

I did know what wine was, but I'd never drunk any.

Later, Mr. Bobalink's son, Young Pete, told me they made Diego Red and if you drank too much, it would make you funny.

While I was at the Bobalink's place, I rode around with Old Pete in his car. On one drive, he asked me if I liked his daughter. Bein' a young man, I didn't know if I liked her or if I was scared of her.

I told him, "I don't even know your daughter."

He told me in his crazy accent, "I a-think a-she'd a-make a-good a-wife, and I a-gib her-a you-a. She's a-good a-cook-a. She a-make a-good a-wine-a too-a. She a-bery good-a girl-a."

I wasn't interested, but I didn't know how to tell Mr. Bobalink that.

Later, when I was talkin' with Young Pete, he told me to pay no attention to his dad since his sister, Anna, had a boyfriend of her own that Old Pete didn't even know about. If Old Pete did know about the boyfriend, Young Pete told me that he'd kill Anna 'cuz he was from the old country and believed in the old way of the parents pickin' the bride or groom for their kids.

That week with the Bobalinks was one of the most enjoyable weeks of my life. Listenin' to him talk and watchin' how he did things was wonderful, and his voice always made me laugh. I guess the long trip, at least 150 miles from Cody to the Bobalink place between Rock Springs and Farson, was worth the three-week long ride just 'cuz I got to meet Mr. Bobalink and learn what a grape and Diego Red was.

Later, Old Pete Bobalink took me into Rock Springs with my horse gear where I waited for a bus to take me back home. Old Pete bought the bus ticket that probably cost about $2. I believe it was the Zanetti Bus line; I know it wasn't Greyhound. Zanetti did run buses across Wyoming for a long time. Since I'd never been on a bus, I was excited to ride somethin' other than a horse. It took at least sixteen hours in that bus from Rock Springs to Wiley, but it was a lot shorter trip than ridin' a horse over that stretch.

For my effort, I got paid twice. Carl Thompson give me $20; he was the one who hired me. Old Pete Bobalink give me $25; he was the one who got the horses. At that time, I was a millionaire, for sure. You'd work like a dog for $1 in the fields, which was the goin' wage at that time, and here, I had $45 to give Mama when I got home from about 22 days of work.

Another funny story growin' up around Cody happened when I was about fourteen or fifteen with a group of my young friends. We were jumpin' the Cody Canal bareback on horses. We were also bare-assed. It was summer; it was hot and we were havin' fun. Why we didn't kill one another, I don't know 'cuz we'd jump in one right after the other on those horses. The canal was 20 feet across and about three to four feet deep up to the horses' withers. We could swim in it even though I didn't know how to swim, but I'd walk and get across someway. We always had fun and I think the horses really enjoyed it too just to get out of the heat.

Anyway, when we were ready to head home, we went over to put our clothes on since we left them on the bank. But there wasn't any damn clothes there, not even our shoes. We were in an awful predicament 'cuz we had to prittin' near ride down the main street of Cody to get home. Stripped buck naked would have been a terrible sight and people would have laughed at us.

At that time, there was a half-assed fence all the way around the town of Cody to keep out livestock and wildlife. We had to get through that fence to get home, so we did it the only way we could—without our clothes.

Funny thing was, when we did get home, our clothes were on the back porch waitin' for us. A group of girls played a trick on us but didn't keep the clothes. Even though Mama had eyes like a hawk, she never saw those sneaky little hussies put our clothes on that porch.

For as hard as life was back then, us kids still had some fun. One day, Carl and I went over to the depot where a great big corral was to hold cattle before shippin' them off on the railroad. In the corral was a big tin shed so the cows could get out of the heat. We found a big rock on the side of the hill that was perfect for rollin', so rollin' it down the hill was our job. We rolled it and it hit the tin shed which scared all the cattle. The cattle broke down the fence and ran all over Cody and across most of Park County. That was fun but made other people work hard to get the cattle back. Us kids just hid up among the boxcars at the depot until things calmed down.

In the wintertime, the road into Meeteetse had a big hill that we would sled down. We called it our "Little Jackson." We had fun 'cuz it was a long hill and our sleds that we guided with our feet sure went fast givin' us big thrills. That was a fun thing to do in those long winter months.

I was still a little kid during another winter when Sid and Edith were courtin'. All three of us went for a ride in an old DeSoto or Nash. I don't know what happened to the car, but Sid got out and looked under the hood while Edith and I stayed inside. Well, when Sid was under there, Edith decided to blast the horn. Sid hit his head on the hood and came out from under there madder than a wet hen and started to spout off. Thankfully, love took ahold of Sid and he forgave Edith so everything was fine. I sure found it comical seein' my brother so mad at his girlfriend.

After we moved to Cody so us kids could go to school, I was real timid. Us, Thayer kids, had never been around lots of other kids or schools, except the little one that Mama ran at Sage Creek. We were shy country kids who had to move to Cody, a pretty good-sized town with at least one thousand people at that time.

None of us were used to other kids teasin' us. Once I came out on the porch of the Cody School, Beatrice Gilmore and Patsy Griever called me, "Redhead, freckle-faced, gingerbread."

Man, I snapped, but I didn't know what to do. Sid came to the school to get us to take us home and he knew what to do about those girls callin' me names.

Sid said, "Beat the hell out of those little bitches."

Those were his exact words and I didn't need to hear 'em twice. I did just what he told me to do. Boy, the tiger came out in my blood right then! After that, I wasn't afraid of any of those town kids—boys or girls.

In 1939, at age 24, I joined the Wyoming National Guard, the 115th Cavalry at Cody. I joined 'cuz I needed enough money to buy Bull Durham tobacco. Young men each got $1 a month to show up for monthly National Guard drills. That was just enough to buy a month's supply of Bull Durham. We rolled our own cigarettes from the 20 sacks that were in a carton, all for $1. One time, my brother Carl and I were running out of Bull Durham and had only a small amount left in the last sack, so we mixed in some horse manure and got along fine with that until we got our next dollar.

In 1941, before Pearl Harbor, the National Guard was inducted into the U.S. Army. Then all of us good men became soldiers. They sent me to Fort Warren in Cheyenne where we got inducted into federal service. From there, they sent me to Fort Leavenworth, Kansas, to get basic training, and then they sent me to Fort Lewis, Washington, and that's when my life changed for the better and forever.

I met Doris, Irene Mitchell on a blind date in St. Helens, Oregon, in early fall of 1943. Dorothy Talley was a friend of Doris' who I'd met at Fort Lewis, and she arranged our date to meet at the St. Helens Café.

Doris pulled up in a 1936 Chevy and I got there on the Fort Lewis military bus. When I got off the bus, I heard a car honk real soft, if you can imagine that. Doris just barely touched the horn. I was the only soldier in uniform on the street that day, so she thought I must be her date, but she wasn't really sure. She was always bashful.

Anyway, we talked a little in the Chevy and I knew right then, within a few seconds, that she was the woman I would marry. I was leery though. One thing crossed my mind that made me hesitate a minute about marriage.

About a month earlier, I walked into the Fort Lewis Military Barracks and saw a young man sitting on his bunk, crying. He really felt bad. Being a corporal in charge of the quarters, I asked him, "What's the matter?"

He told me, "You don't really want to know."

I told him I did want to know, and he started to tell me his sad story. He had gotten married but had never met the woman's parents before they married. Him, being a Southern boy from Georgia, had strong beliefs and when he did meet his new bride's parents, he found out they were both colored people. He showed me a picture of his bride who was very nice-lookin' and had blond hair.

He said, "In this situation, I either lose my parents or lose her."

I told him this situation was plumb out of my category, but I would arrange for him to see the chaplain.

I went over and told the sergeant the story. The sergeant then got in touch with the chaplain who came right over to the barracks. In a short time, the chaplain had the marriage declared null and void.

I was thinkin' about that story when Doris asked me if I wanted to meet her folks. Honestly, I hadn't told her the Georgia boy's story yet, so I went to meet her folks. I liked them a lot right away. I could have gone through hell-and-a-half acre, but I would never have gotten better in-laws. They were wonderful people, down-to-earth folks.

Sometimes, I wonder if that Georgia boy and his bride would have been happy together. Ain't it somethin' how skin color makes us react even if it hurts us?

Doris and I never made it into the St. Helens Café. We prittin' near went straight to see her folks, Clarence and Elma Mitchell, at their home outside St. Helens. Her dad became my dad right on the spot; he was a wonderful man, so nice. I decided right then that I was going to try to hang on to this gal and I did.

We visited that night and Clarence told me about the logging business. He said, "We snake the logs out with a mule. Snakin' means to pull them out."

Since I knew a lot about snakes and a little about mules, I asked him how big his mules were.

He said, "They're various sizes. But they can pull logs that are 60 feet long and four feet in diameter."

I thought to myself, this guy stretches stories 'cuz I never saw a mule big enough to haul that kind of load. I wanted to go a bit further with him about the mules, so I asked again, "How big were the mules?"

He said again, "They are different sizes. They can pull anything as long as you feed them wood."

I knew he was crazy, then, 'cuz I sure knew enough to know mules don't eat wood. It finally came out that the "mules" he was talkin' about were steam engines used in the loggin' business. Here, me, kinda a cowboy type, always thought mules had four legs.

Mr. Mitchell, Doris's dad, was pretty interestin'. When he was a young man, his aunt in Michigan ran a jewelry store and she took him in to learn that business. He didn't like that business, so he went from there to be a cabinet maker and he was a mighty good one when he moved from Michigan to Oregon. When he got to Oregon, funny thing was, he met a cabinet maker from Michigan who gave him a job. Eventually, my father-in-law made my cabinets in the first house Doris and I built. But I'm gettin' ahead of myself.

Anyway, Doris's mother was adopted, and we don't know much about her childhood. Elma and Clarence met in Michigan but couldn't afford to be married then, so Clarence moved to Oregon and sent Elma money to come later. They were married in Oregon. Elma was a good wife and a good mother to their four children—Heloise, Doris born on November 17, 1918, Alice, and Glen. Elma was a really good cook too. My wife took after her.

Doris and I knew each other about 36 hours in total before we got married in Kelso, Washington, by a Catholic priest. Doris's folks came with us along with their son, Glen. Since my Mama died in 1941 and Dad was gone long before then, they didn't know anything about Doris. None of my family in Wyoming could have made a weddin' in Washington in those days anyway 'cuz of the war.

Doris was a great worker. Before we married, she was a librarian in St. Helens where a lady there taught her to play the piano. She was really good at it but wouldn't play in front of people, even me, 'cuz she was so shy. During the war, she worked in the Bemus Bag Company at their St. Helens factory where they made paper bags.

Doris was a wonderful wife too. She made great meals, canned all kinds of food and always kept a nice house. She also liked to work in the garden. Years later, she helped me run our meat business where she kept the books, wrapped the meat, helped clean up the shop, and never complained even though it was tough work sometimes. It was good work for Doris 'cuz she was shy and didn't have to talk with a lot of people to get the job done.

Doris was a wonderful mother. We had four kids. They were all successful in their lives in Oregon and Nevada. We lost our youngest in 1976 to a ranching accident when he was haulin' irrigation pipe that hit an electric power line. That was the most awful thing in our marriage, but we came through. It still makes me sad; Doris was really sad too. No one knows how sad it is until it happens to them.

Here are a couple of funny stories about Doris. We were riding the railroad comin' back to Wyoming for the funeral of my oldest brother, Bugs, around 1948 or '49. We left our boys with their grandparents in

St. Helens. Comin' into Butte, Montana, Doris looked out the window and saw a big "B" painted white on a hill.

She asked me, "What's that?"

I told her it snowed letters on hills in Butte.

When we came back on the train from the funeral, she looked up and saw the same letter "B." She said, "I guess it don't get very warm here 'cuz that snow hasn't melted."

That's when I gave her the name "Dude," which I called her most of the time in our marriage. She was a dude 'cuz she didn't know the difference between Butte snow and painted "B" letters. Still makes me smile to think of that trip.

Once, we were drivin' from Oregon to Wyoming for a vacation I had comin' from the paper mill. Our youngest hadn't been born yet, but the other three kids were with Doris and me. The kids wanted to sleep outside, so I parked our '51 Buick alongside the road one evening.

We took our sleepin' bags out of the car and just laid them in the alfalfa field nearby. We didn't put up a tent or any shelter since it was a nice night. Then, about dark, here the mosquitos come by the millions and ruined the nice night.

To top it all off, my daughter didn't want to stay in bed. She wanted to crawl around in the alfalfa field. Then I'd have to pull her back in the sleepin' bag with me. She always liked sleepin' with me when she was little and I loved smellin' her sweet blond hair. You know how little puppies smell so sweet. Little kids smell that way sometimes too, especially my daughter. I just loved that smell.

The next morning, we got up and were rollin' up our sleepin' bags when a woman came across the field, wavin' a dishrag at us. I told Doris and the kids to get in the Buick and I would take care of whatever she wanted. It was the easiest thing I ever took care of in my life.

The woman invited all of us over for breakfast. She had seen the kids in the alfalfa field and felt sorry for them sleepin' outside. I told her the kids wanted to sleep out there. All of us had lots of mosquito bites, but the kids looked like they had measles. That woman taught me a new cure. She put a mouthwash, something like Listerine, on a cloth to dab on the kids' mosquito bites and within a few hours they were gone so you could barely see them anymore.

We all sure liked the breakfast too. To say thanks to these nice people, I helped her husband haul two tons of hay. They were wonderful people. In those days, we all helped each other.

After 64 years of marriage, the love of my life died on March 15, 2009, at age 90 in Cody, Wyoming. That was the same day as Doris's sister, Heloise's, birthday. I couldn't even tell Heloise about Doris's death 'cuz she was sick and I was sick with sadness too. Doris is buried in Lander, Wyoming, next to our son in Mount Hope Cemetery. I make weekly visits to their gravesites and will be buried by them too one day.

Durin' our life together, we had many adventures and challenges. We also had lots of opportunities. One opportunity was for me to invent two devices that could help others or save their lives. Around 1951, I got a patent for an automatic fire alarm. It ran by clockworks. What triggered it off was a soft lead wire tied onto the ringer of the clock. When the heat got warm enough, the lead would melt and make the ringer start ringin'. It cost about $8-9 per alarm to make, but I didn't manufacture them. I sold my patent to a fire alarm company that didn't want any competition, so they bought my invention. They eventually sold out to another company, and my product never made it to market.

Another invention was a safety stirrup. It was a stirrup that would never let you get hung up on a horse. I got the patent for this invention in the 1980s. The top of the stirrup would release if you could put enough pressure from your toes to the top of the stirrup to pop it open. There was no extra strap from the saddle like you have with most stirrups. This stirrup went right into the saddle's skirt and worked like a swivel if you ever got in trouble. I sold the stirrup patent to a saddle company from Texas. They didn't want competition either since they mostly sold regular stirrups. But that product of mine didn't make it to market either.

I learned a lot from all this livin' and inventin'. Big companies don't give a shit, and most people are hard to change. One man told me the stirrup idea was really great since it could save lives, but no cowboy would ever buy it. He said I'd have more chances sellin' a cowboy a helmet instead of a cowboy hat than to get him to buy a new kind of stirrup. People don't want to change, no matter how good an idea is.

George and Florence Thayer near Old Arland,
Wyoming, c. 1899 *(Thayer family photo)*

George Thayer Freight Line hauling wool with sixteen
horses, c. 1900 *(Thayer family photo)*

Long Hollow School, c. 1900, Florence and Annie
Fenton, far left. (*Thayer family photo*)

Left to right, Jack Fenton, Bob Fenton. Fenton,
Wyoming, c. 1880 *(Thayer family photo)*

Left to right, Florence, Bob, Annie Fenton. Fenton,
Wyoming, c. 1880 *(Thayer family photo)*

George "Bugs" Thayer, c. 1936 *(Thayer family photo)*

Frank Lundie, Meeteetse Sheriff, Rock Springs,
Wyoming, c. 1894 *(Thayer family photo)*

Florence "Flossy" Thayer, Lundie's Mother, c. 1927 *(Thayer family photo)*

CHAPTER 2

Animals

First off, I want you to know that I was always taught to take good care of my animals. My whole family taught me about animals 'cuz we depended on them for food and transportation. Granddad was really strict about takin' care of horses, especially his work horses. One day, I came in from rakin' hay when I was just a small boy. I put the team of two horses in the barn, fed them their hay and headed to the house to eat my dinner. There was other ranch hands comin' to eat too. When we all got to the table, we ate a wonderful dinner. All the time, I had my eye on dessert—my favorite bread puddin' that Grandma always made. I finished my meal and Grandpa finished his. Then he reached over and grabbed my dish of bread puddin' and ate it. Man, that was a heartbreaker.

When he got done eatin' my dessert, he wiped his moustache and said, "Lundie, I had to feed oats to your horses. So, therefore, I got your puddin'. You know horses get hay and oats."

My heart was broken, but I went back out to get my team to start rakin' hay again. Pretty soon, Grandma came out and gave me some sugar cookies. She told me, "That will take the place of the bread puddin'." It was our secret. She was a great grandma.

I have lots of animal stories from a long time ago, but I'll tell you some recent stories too. One day, I went to town with my friend, Karen. She took me to a doctor's appointment and then we stopped at the grocery store in Lander for some supplies. I stayed in the car with her little black Scottie dog for a little while—until he jumped out of the window that Karen left open. I tried to catch him, but all I got was a couple of hairs out of his tail. So, I got out of the car to catch that rascal.

It was funny that all this happened on the main street in downtown Lander and lots of people saw us. For a short-legged dog, he could surely run. I took off after him runnin' as fast as I could for a 98 year-old man. A long-legged teenage boy saw me tryin' to catch that dog and decided he'd help. Well, that little dog outran him too and kept runnin' down the street where lots of cars were stoppin' to try to head him off. Pretty soon, I gave up and went back to the car to face Karen, who I knew was gonna be real upset.

Karen came out of the store and I told her what happened. Boom! She took off runnin' to find that dog. Pretty soon, she gave up too and came back to the car. We were standin' in that parkin' lot tryin' to figure out what we would do next. All of a sudden, here came two young ladies with that Scottie dog on a leash. Karen and I were so happy to see him. We thanked the ladies a lot and put the dog back in the car after we both made double sure the windows were up. I think that was the last time I ran that fast and I didn't feel very good either. It was probably about 90 years since I ran that fast.

We still laugh at that story thinkin' about how many people saw me runnin' down the main street after a little dog. Lots of people tried to help me 'cuz they probably thought, "Oh, that poor old man. He must be crazy."

Well, maybe I am crazy. After all that runnin' around, I changed the dog's name. Karen called him Roy, but now we both call him Greyhound.

I love animals so much that I think the horse should be the national animal. You think about a horse a minute. We would not have this country without horses. They were the only transportation us pioneers ever had back then and the country would never have been settled without them. I think the whole nation needs to recognize how much the horse contributed to this country.

Right now, I don't have a horse, but I have a wonderful cat. His name is Partner and he sure is a good one. Karen gave him to me 'cuz my dog got killed and she knows I love pets. Partner plays hide-and-seek and peek-a-boo around the house with me. No kiddin'. He'll peek around a corner and when I move just a little, he'll take off.

One morning, he tried to get me to eat mice since that's what he brought me for breakfast in bed. Another afternoon, I was sittin' with the door open 'cuz it was nice and sunny. I was dozin' off, and all at once, Partner attacked me. I didn't know what was happenin' since he'd been so friendly before. Well, he was after a mouse and, believe it or not, that mouse had run up my pant leg. Partner must have been stalkin' him, so he jumped on me to get to the mouse.

When I felt the mouse crawlin' up my leg, I didn't know what it was since I never had a mouse in my pants before. Anyway, I grabbed that mouse through my pant leg and squished him good. When I jumped up, the mouse fell out of my pants onto the floor. Partner grabbed it and started to play with the dead thing but never did eat it.

Since Partner was born wild, he'd never had a home before Karen brought him to me. So he ate plenty of mice to survive, I guess. But now that he is civilized, he likes cat food and milk and just plays with mice, dead or alive. He sure is a wonderful partner to me but not to any mouse.

Years before Partner came, I stepped outside one mornin', and it was real cold. Lo and behold, somethin' flew over my head. I thought it was a parakeet. I didn't know what to tell my wife about it 'cuz she would have thought I had lost my cuckoo for sure. Anyway, I came back into the house and ate breakfast with my wife before I went back outside again to do chores.

This time, I looked up on the garage roof, and there sat a cockatiel! It was a cold February morning in Wyoming, and on the roof of my garage was a tropical bird, honest. I took a ladder and a snow rake and got up on the roof. Believe it or not, that cockatiel crawled right onto the end of the rake. I was on the ladder, but I brought the snow rake with the cockatiel slow and low toward my wife who was watchin' the whole thing from the ground. That bird, swear to God, walked right onto my wife's hand. You bet, Doris took him straight into the house.

You know something? That bird was really tame. Doris sat him on a back of a chair and he just sat there for several minutes. He was probably really glad to finally get warm. Who knows how long that bird had been outside? I called around and talked with neighbors, but no one had a cockatiel or knew anyone who did, so we knew he wasn't from these parts. We figured he probably got loose from a truck driver since they sometimes have mascots in their trucks. We had no indoor bird supplies, so I had to go to town and get him a cage, food, and toys. That bird lived with us for four or five years before he got the croup and died. I think that's the only inside bird I ever had and he just arrived one snowy February morning.

Back to the reason I think horses should be our national animal is 'cuz I've owned several really good saddle horses. One of them I'll tell you about was named Baldy, a beautiful dark bay with a bald face and four stockin' feet. He was the most honest horse I ever rode and he won me some money too. I was a young man, probably sixteen or seventeen, when Baldy became my horse. Once, I was drivin' a bunch of cattle that we had to deliver to Sam Riley. Old Baldy and I drove those cattle from Cody to the other side of Meeteetse, about 30 miles.

After the cattle were delivered, on my way back toward Cody, I went into Meeteetse instead of cuttin' cross-country. The next day was gonna be Labor Day and Meeteetse people always had a big Labor Day celebration that they still have today, I think. I went out to the Meeteetse rodeo grounds and was watching the calf ropin' event while sitting on Baldy. We were both kind of restin' up for the rest of our trip back to Cody when a man called Evie Robertson came up behind us and honked his car horn. Baldy let loose and knocked a headlight right out with one of his hind legs.

All Mr. Robertson said was, "He's a frisky little bugger."

After that, I put Baldy into the cowboy race and we won. We also won the Free-For-All Race that let prittin' near anyone race even on a mule or a cat if it would carry you. But, most people just used horses.

Evie Robertson, unknown to me, had a thoroughbred stallion that he'd gotten from Mr. Ur. Well, Mr. Robertson entered his stallion in the race that only pure-bred horses could. That year, the race was gonna be cancelled 'cuz there weren't any competitors, just Mr. Robertson's horse.

My brother, Sid, came to me and said, "Do you think you and Baldy could beat that stud?"

I told Sid, "I'll give it a hell of a try."

Sid asked Mr. Robertson if he would run his horse against Baldy.

Mr. Robertson told Sid, "Well, that would be a cinch. Have you got any money to bet on it?"

Sid told him he had $90 to wager.

Mr. Robertson told Sid, "OK, the race is on if you put up the $90."

My brother reached in his hip pocket and pulled out the money, askin', "Where's your $90, Evie?"

Evie said that he could be trusted, but Sid said, "You put yours up and I'll put mine up. We'll get someone else to hold the stakes until the race is over."

Sid gave the money to Rufus Wilson to hold until the winner was known. We didn't have announcers or cameras or anything like today, but we had honest people and good livestock.

The Meeteetse "Race Track" was just a dirt road around a bunch of sagebrush without any fence or markers. There was a finish line which was only some chalk in the dirt. The races were all run in a circle, but we didn't have a judge or anything to tell who the winner was. The community could see for themselves who crossed the finish line first. Well, they all saw me and Baldy cross that finish line at least seven horse lengths ahead of that thoroughbred. I do believe the other horse would have won that race if he'd ever been raced in sagebrush before. That day, the thoroughbred didn't know how to handle himself. He couldn't concentrate on our kind of race track. Hell's fire, Baldy knew all about runnin' through sagebrush.

Another wonderful horse I had later for several years was named Pilot. He was a big, gray horse that I could rope anything on and he could handle 'em. For his size, he was very fast. Since he was a stud, he was also very stubborn. He didn't like water. Honest to God, if we crossed a stream that was one inch across, that horse had to clear it by 30 feet. You better be ready and watchin' him or you'd land on the ground. We sure got a lot of good colts out of Pilot and some big adventures.

One day, my son, Mark, was helpin' me drive our cows up the mountain above Fort Washakie. I wanted to take a bull up too, but the bull had crossed the North Fork and I had to go get him before we headed up the mountain. Well, Pilot blew up when I tried to cross the river that was really rollin' big that year. I went flyin' off and had to dive under a barbed wire fence that was across the river before I could get back to land. Pilot went plumb under the water too. Then he stood up and just shook his head before he went right back to Mark. Only trouble was, I was on the other side of the river.

Mark went to the house and told Doris what happened. Doris called my brother, Charlie, who lived pretty close to us. Charlie came over to help get Pilot and me together so we could get the cows and that bull up the mountain.

I sat behind Charlie on his horse as we crossed the river to get back to Pilot. When we got to him, Charlie snubbed Pilot up real close to his horse so that Pilot wouldn't try to jump again. We went safely back across the river, Charlie on his horse and me on Pilot snubbed up real tight.

Then, we all tried to get the bull back with the herd. Well, when that bull saw us comin' toward him, he jumped right into that fast-flowin' river and just rolled over and over in the water. All you could see was his belly and then his back before he went way on downstream.

Charlie said, "Well, Pete, that's the last of your bull."

Charlie snubbed me and Pilot up again and we headed back across the river to the herd of cows without the bull. When he got to the herd, I couldn't believe it, and neither could Charlie, but that bull was back with the herd. We never figured out how he did it either since both banks of the river were pretty steep.

Another little incident about Pilot was when we were on top of the mountain lookin' for cows. We were on the North Fork River, comin' up the trail, when I saw a mama beaver and four or five little beavers workin' on a log. Well, sure enough, they fell that log right across the trail. I knew that Pilot would go ape if he saw those beavers, so I grabbed hold of the saddle horn to get ready for a wild ride. Just as soon as we got around a tree, the beavers evidently saw us first and they just went splash, splash, and splash right back in the water.

Thank God, the beavers went back in the water 'cuz I wasn't ready to be a bronc rider or a swimmer again that day. Boy, that sucker Pilot could sure buck. He was a real good horse, but he wasn't trustworthy like Baldy or Velvet. I brought Pilot with us to Wyoming from Oregon where there was always a lot of water, but he sure didn't like Wyoming water. I don't know what was the matter with him.

I do know another wonderful horse that I bought at the Lander Stockyards. He was a quarter horse that was brought into Wyoming from somewhere in Colorado. The man that was showin' him in the ring that day, slid off the horse's back, picked up all four legs, and did anything he wanted to that beautiful sorrel horse. I said to myself that I'd have to get the money since I wanted to buy that horse 'cuz he was nice and gentle, just perfect for my youngest son. We bought him and brought him home. The next mornin', I went out to take my first ride on him.

He went ape-shit when I went to put the saddle on him. I could see right there that the horse had been doped up in the ring to make him so calm the day before. I finally got him in the corner of the corral, got on board, and we went for a little ride. He tried to buck, but I held him up owin' to the way I had the halter and everything fixed.

Later, I learned the only way that horse would turn was always to the right. To teach him to turn left, I took him up on the river and headed into a thick bunch of willows. I kept turnin' him left away from the willows until he learned he could turn both ways. He wouldn't have ever turned that way before I learnt him. I figured whoever rode that horse only turned right on him. They probably had him tied to an exercise machine or wheel that only turned one way and that was to the right. I rode him for a couple of days which was the fastest I ever broke a horse. A few days later, my son got on him and they got along just fine.

Turns out that horse was really smart and honest. He would do everything and anything to please you. You could rope off him and he'd get you right where you needed to be to catch a cow or whatever. He wanted to make you happy, you could just tell. He had a real smooth gait which is why we named him Velvet. He lived to be 34 years old and was always a wonderful horse. He's buried near my place on Boulder Flats.

When I was a teenage boy, there was a tight wad named Mr. Molsworth who lived in Cody. Now, he ran a furniture store there and if you ever find a piece of furniture at an auction sale with the name Molesworth on it, you'd be wise to nab it no matter what it cost.

Anyway, a bunch of us kids were out peelin' white and red cedar for Mr. Molesworth to make furniture with. We were sittin' outside his store on a nice day eatin' lunch. Here comes Mr. DeMoriak drivin' up the street in a Packard car. Both Molesworth and DeMoriak were really wealthy people and so they talked a lot with each other. That day, they were talkin' outside near where us kids were eatin' our lunch. Right then, a rooster flew out of nowhere and landed on the fence. On one side of the fence was his pen and on the other side was the street.

Mr. Molesworth had chickens and roosters, but we hadn't seen any of them that day. Mr. Molesworth said, "I'll bet you $50 that rooster flies into the street."

Mr. DeMoriak said, "I'll call you. I bet he flies right back into his pen."

Lo and behold, that rooster flew right back in his pen and Mr. Molesworth lost $50 which wasn't a whole lot of money to those men but to us kids it was a fortune, especially since Mr. Molesworth only paid us kids 10¢ an hour to peel that cedar. Of course, we were happy to get any money and 80¢ a day was good wages for us.

When I was still just a teenage kid, I went to a horse race I remember real good. Old Nick Knight was a famous world champion saddle bronc rider and he was entered in the Cody Stampede.

Nick said, "Hey, Pete, put your horse in the wild horse corral and I'll pick him to race in the wild horse race. He really looks wild with that long mane and tail."

I had taken Diamond, a real gentle bay with a white diamond on his forehead, but I hadn't curried him or brushed him since we just brought him in off the range that day. He had cockle burrs in his tail and mane and looked really wild. Well, I knew Diamond wasn't a wild horse and so did Nick, but I put him in with the wild horses and Nick entered the Wild Horse Race.

Nick got on Diamond and they ran all the way around the track until about three hundred feet from the finish line. The band struck up to cheer on the winner since he was the world champion and a Cody boy. Just like the band struck up, old Diamond struck up too and bucked Nick plumb off. Diamond bucked off a world champion but was the gentlest horse really. He'd never heard a brass band before, of course, he had to kick up his heels. Yep, Diamond became world champion that day and turned around runnin' back the wrong way. It still makes me laugh to think about it.

Another story about the Knight family doesn't make me laugh. It's really sad. Nick's brothers, Tom and George, were headin' as fast they could to Red Lodge, Montana, for the night rodeo up there. They didn't know that a Caterpillar tractor had gone off the road and there was a cable across the road that was bein' used to haul the tractor back up. Well, sure enough, those boys hit that cable goin' at a good clip and it cut every one of them right in two.

The officials had the Knight boys' vehicle hauled to Thermopolis and displayed in front of everybody to show the kids what high speeds can do to a person's body. There was blood and mess all over and the cable had just sheared off the top of the vehicle. Too bad, but maybe someone learned a lesson.

The Knight family had another tragedy too. Tom and George's sister was named Hilda. She ran the Needle Back Hot Springs Plunge in Cody mostly for the tourists. One day, her little girl came up missin'. Everyone looked for that little girl up and down the river, out in the sagebrush, and even posted her disappearance with a national radio show that helped locate lost kids.

Well, three or four months went by with no word about the little girl. Finally, someone hiked up the hills to a cliff above the Plunge and saw something on the Plunge's roof. It looked like a skeleton. When they finally checked it out, sure enough, it was Hilda's little girl who had apparently fallen off the cliff and landed on the Plunge roof, but no one thought to look there.

They were a great family that got along real good with our family. Their dad was a rodeo hand who always liked watchin' us kids get bucked off of goats, sheep, horses, or whatever we were tryin' to ride. All the kids were good cowboys too, but they sure had a lot of tragedy. Back in those days, tragedy came around a lot to almost every family.

The Cody Stampede was a real old rodeo even when I was a kid. It started long before I did and it still goes on today. I can remember the announcer, Milward Simpson, and how he'd open every rodeo night. He'd say, "I'm wild and wooly and full of fleas. I've not been curried above the knees, but I'll make it into Cody for the next stampede." All the people liked that jingle, and I still remember it.

One rodeo night, there was a Wild Cow Milkin' Contest. I mean to tell you those cows were plumb wild and mean. Can't remember his last name, but Harold, a friend of mine, told me, "Hey, Pete, let's enter that milkin' contest. I've got a plan, so we'll win it."

I asked, "What's your big idea this time?"

He said, "I'll rope the cow and you milk her. Now, I'll tell you how we're gonna win. You get a big mouthful of milk before we line up in front of the judges to show them our empty milk bottles. If they say anything to you, just swallow the milk."

Well, they didn't say a word to either of us. They just looked at the bottles, so Harold roped a wild cow that was a mean SOB too. When Harold got her settled down, I stuck my head in her flank to start to milk her and to make sure the judges couldn't see what I was about to do.

The minute I spit the milk I had in my mouth into the milk bottle, I knew we were winners. I grabbed the milk bottle and ran like hell to the judges and showed them the milk in the bottle. We got first place that day and split the $5 prize between us.

By the way, Harold was ridin' Baldy when he roped that wild cow. Shows you how good a horse Baldy was and shows you what little sneaks us kids were back then.

When I was a young man, I was walkin' down a Cody street and a man I knew named Gus Dodge came up to me and said, "You want a job, Lundie?"

I said yes prittin' near before he even got my name out of his mouth.

He took me to the Hot Foot Dude Ranch up the South Fork River about 15 or 20 miles from Cody. Gus told me he wanted me to mow his hay and put it up, so I told him I'd do it. Back in those days, I'd do just about anything for some money 'cuz the Depression was really hard on us ranch folks.

A little girl lived at the Hot Foot Dude Ranch at the time. Her name was Cissy, I think. Cissy had two Great Dane dogs named Moose and Sooner. They were beautiful dogs, but they kept gettin' in front of the mowin' machine. I knew what they were after. They were gettin' the mice that the mower tossed up.

I kept askin' Cissy to keep her dogs away from the mower, but she wouldn't do it. And I couldn't get after her 'cuz those dogs would have taken care of me. Gee, they were great big dogs. Well, sure enough, old Sooner got in front of the sickle. I couldn't stop in time. Sooner lost two toes.

I tied the team up and Cissy and the dogs followed me toward the house. I told her to stay outside and take care of Sooner. Pretty soon, Gus came up and asked why I quit mowin' hay and I told him what happened. Right then, the boss lady came out and told me and Gus that I was fired.

Gus said, "Before you fire him, you better look at Sooner's toes."

I told her that I'd asked Cissy several times to get the dogs away and she wouldn't do what I asked.

She looked at Sooner's foot and then took a rope, put it around Cissy's belly, and tied her to the porch.

She told me, "I'm sorry, Lundie. I didn't know the circumstances."

After that, I went back to mowin' hay. Every meal I ate at that house from then on, Cissy was tied up. Bein' tied up didn't stop her from stickin' her tongue out at me every day though. Years later, when I was comin' through Cody on furlough, I ran into that boss lady at a dance hall called Wolfville. She greeted me, and with her was a beautiful young woman. Sure enough, it was Cissy all growed up. She gave me a big hug, but all I could see was her still stickin' her tongue out at me.

My Uncle Bob and Grandma told me about one day when they were out ridin' to check the cows on the Fenton place with Granddad. They came up on a mare that was havin' a colt. The colt was halfway out, but the mare couldn't push it out the rest of the way. It's hard to believe, but that mare was dead and the colt was still alive and tryin' to be born.

The men pulled the colt out. But, after a while, the colt still seemed weak.

Uncle Bob said, "I pulled my pistol out and was about to shoot the colt, but your Granddad said, 'Oh no, you don't.'"

Granddad told Uncle Bob, "I'm gonna keep that colt."

Granddad rode about six miles back to the ranch, got the buggy, and then took it back those same six miles so he could get the colt home in it.

Meanwhile, back at the ranch, there was a work mare that had lost her colt a few days earlier and she accepted the orphaned colt. Granddad named that colt Foal, which was an interestin' name for a horse that should never have been born. When that colt grew up, it was one of my Granddad's favorite saddle horses.

Later in life, Uncle Bob married Ruth and they had Buster, Milly, Lyla Pearl, Charlie, and Ruth who all grew up on the Fenton place. One day, Buster and I wanted to go ridin', but we only had Old

Shorty, the horse I was ridin', in the corral while Buster's horse was still in the pasture. She was a mean mare, the herd boss that put many a person out of the pasture. She was more like a stud and ruled over all the mares and geldings.

I got a piece of chain about three to four feet long and rode Shorty out in the pasture. When we came on the mare, I slapped her in the jaw with the chain. She ran back over to the herd. I rode over, put a rope around her neck and led her into the corral. Buster never had trouble catchin' her again. You could catch that horse anywhere after that. Kinda funny that a horse never forgets anything; smarter than a lot of people that way.

Here's a sad horse story. I was a teenager when I went to the Cody Stockyards where there were close to six hundred head of horses. A horse buyer had bought them from various ranchers, and they were gonna be shipped to Butte, Montana, for dog food.

I was just lookin' at all those horses when I spotted the most beautiful colored animal that I'd ever seen in my life. He was a color between a chestnut sorrel and a palomino. Almost like the color of a really light penny—not copper or brass but somewhere in between. Beautiful, I've never seen that color of horse ever again.

I really wanted to buy that colt, but the horse buyer said he wanted $5 for him. There was no way I had $5 in those days. My oldest brother, Bugs, was with me and he had about $1. A couple of other people we knew were there that day and they had some money too, but we couldn't come up with $5 to buy that colt. That was one of the saddest times in my life. I watched that colt go up the chute into the stock car and I knew what was gonna happen to him. Man, that was so sad.

I cried and Bugs told me, "That's part of being a man."

There's some parts of being a man that I don't like. I remember that colt from that day to this.

Oh yeah. I had a horse once that really took me for a ride. When I was breakin' him as a three-year-old, Bugs and I took him out for a ride one day. Bugs was ridin' my horse's mother who was a really good runner.

Bugs said to me, "I wonder if that colt can run."

I said, "I dunno."

Bugs said, "Well, let's give him a try."

Now, when I break a horse, I take the halter and tie it real tight to the saddle horn. The horse can still move its head side-to-side, but it can't put its head down and buck you off. When Bugs challenged me to a race, I loosened the halter's lead rope and said, "Let's go."

We went alright. We ran that race on the new Cody Airport landing strip. There were no planes around for hundreds of miles, so Bugs and I thought it was a good race track.

Now, don't let anyone tell you that a horse can't buck when it's runnin' wide open. I'm livin' proof they can. My horse was called Hell's Bells and did he live up to his name that day. He flipped his lid while we were runnin' wide open and I went airborne. Even though Cody had no airplanes, I was airborne until I crashed.

I landed on my back and skidded on that gravel for at least 30-40 feet. Bugs turned around and asked if I was hurt.

I really thought I had broken my back, but all I had was a whole lot of gravel stuck in my skin. My shirt was torn completely off. Bugs said to take the mare and he'd ride Hell's Bells home.

When we got home, Mama, my sisters, my brothers, and anyone else who wanted to help started pickin' the gravel out of my back. They worked on me for several hours off and on until they thought they had all of it. As the days went by, they'd keep pickin' more out since they missed some at different times.

Years later, when I was in the military, I developed a lump on my back amid all the scars that Hell's Bells give me. I went to the army doctor who told me he was gonna remove the lump. When he cut into it, lo and behold, there was a rock about the size of the end of my little finger that we had missed all those years earlier.

The doctor wanted to know about all my scars and I told him, "Hell's Bells give 'em to me."

Now, another story about the Cody Airport will set the record straight. I was the first person to ever land on the Cody Airport airstrip, but Bill Monday and Amelia Earhart flew real airplanes into that airport. They were the first two airplanes to ever land there. It was said for sure that Bill Monday could land an airplane anywhere. I'm not sure but that's the story I heard.

After I landed on the Cody Airstrip, I tended camp up on Dead Indian Mountain and in Butter Bowl Basin where I saw some wonderful animal sights. Baby mountain sheep would come down and play with the domestic lambs while the adult mountain sheep would lick salt with the tame sheep. It was fun to watch them run, buck, and play. Imagine one thousand head of wild and domestic critters playin' with each other.

This is a funny animal story about pigs and horses, well, really a donkey. There was a man who lived in Cody. He had blond hair and the blondest beard I've ever seen. His name was Donkey Smith. I don't know how he got the name, but that's what some people called him. Most people called him Mr. Smith and everyone knew he loved his pigs.

He also loved his son who was named Summer Smith who looked just like Donkey, same color of hair and beard. You'd swear to Christ they were twins. When they both got older, Summer lived in Idaho and came to Cody one day to take Donkey back to Idaho with him.

Donkey didn't want to go 'cuz he couldn't take his money with him. When Donkey went to the Cody Bank to withdraw his money, the bank told him they would transfer the money to a bank in Idaho. Donkey didn't like that idea at all and wanted his money, around $50,000 in cash that very day from that very bank. In those days, $50,000 was like $50 million in these days. Finally, Summer convinced Donkey to transfer the money to Idaho.

For the trip, Donkey bought two teams of Percheron horses. One team pulled the personal belongings and supplies. The other team pulled their trailer house, but in those days, we called 'em sheep wagons. They made their way through Yellowstone Park and when they got back to Idaho, Summer wrote Mama a letter to thank us for helpin' his dad. Summer also said in the letter that Donkey wanted Sid to be sure to take care of his pigs, so Sid bought all the pigs and the pig pen and lived at Donkey's place for a while.

Donkey loved his pigs so much they all lived together in the pig house when Donkey was still in Cody. Donkey would eat his meals and then scrape the scraps right into the pig trough beside him. But, Donkey Smith would also haul garbage from wherever he could find it to feed those pigs. His main garbage spot was the depot at the hotel by the railroad track.

One day, Donkey had four barrels of garbage. Listen, those were 50 gallon barrels too, full of slop that he was haulin' from the hotel to his pigs. Goin' up a hill, one of the horses balked and would not move. Now, Donkey always smoked a pipe, so he raised the horse's tail up and stuck his pipe under the tail to get the horse a-movin'. Boy did that horse move!

That team of horses ran away and scattered garbage all up and down the main street of Cody. Cody citizens had to volunteer to take the fire hoses out on the streets and wash 'em up. Donkey Smith was told that he couldn't haul any more garbage down the main street any longer. Yep, Donkey Smith still kept feedin' his pigs slop that he hauled by takin' back streets.

The main street of Cody wasn't paved but all gravel. I mean, gravel over an inch around was all that made that street. As a young boy, my buddies and I would go to war against one another and our ammunition was not gravel but horse turds. The Cody City Council passed an ordinance, believe it or not, that us kids couldn't have any more horse turd wars 'cuz, once in a while, a rock would get picked up with the turd and get tossed that would break out a window. None of us kids got convicted, but sometimes we got hit with a rock.

I loved dogs as much as I did my horses. One of the most amazing dogs I ever knew belonged to Mr. Tom Oliver. The dog's name was Jigs and fondly nicknamed Jiggers. Tom thought the world of Jigs to the point that Jigs got the same food as Tom. Now, Tom was a sheepherder and Jigs helped earn their keep, so Tom figured Jiggers could eat as good as him. Jigs was terrible smart. I'll tell you about two incidents with Jigs and Tom.

Once, I was packin' horses up on Dead Indian Mountain outside Cody. It was fall and we were bringin' the sheep off the mountain. I went ahead with the horses and came into a little park—open space. There was a great big herd of sheep, at least two thousand head, grazin'. On the far side of the flock sat a man. I rode over, and lo and behold, it was Tom Oliver who I had known for a long time. Tom knew me when I was just a little snot-nosed kid.

I told Tom, "I've got at least another two thousand head of sheep comin' up the trail, headin' to this park. What are we gonna do to keep our herds from mixin'?"

Tom calmly said, "My Jiggers will take care of them."

I was still standin' by Tom when my flock showed up. Tom just pointed his finger at Jigs and Jigs took off to keep the flocks separated. He just kept movin' between the two flocks, keepin' them lined out the way they were supposed to be. When Beaver, my sheepherder, brought the herd out of the woods, Jigs met 'em and just walked between the two herds. Beaver simply took my herd around Tom's and we had no problems at all. Imagine almost four thousand head of sheep and only one dog to keep them all straight. Jigs was really smart and so was Tom.

Now, I'll tell you the other incident about Tom and Jigs. Tom came to Cody and, of course, Jigs was always with him. Jigs was a pretty animal—a mix between Border Collie and St. Bernard, stood about two feet from the ground and was tan and white. He didn't take after the St. Bernard side since he wasn't real big, only about medium-sized. Tom pampered Jigs and made his Jiggers a bed all his own. It was made of two sheep hides that were sewn together with full-fleece, which means it was about three or four inches thick. Tom always took Jigs' bed along with them wherever they went.

Before he went into a restaurant one night, Tom got a little pie-eyed. As he opened the door, he said, "Come on, Jiggers. Let's eat."

He ordered up two T-bone steaks with all the trimmin's. One was for him, and the other was for Jigs. When the steaks came, Tom put Jigs' meal on the floor.

The waitress had a fit, sayin', "You can't feed that dog in here. Get him out!"

Tom responded, "I paid for his T-bone steak. I paid for mine. He's gonna eat it in here just like I am."

Well, the waitress called the police. When they arrived, the police asked what the problem was. She said, "Tom won't take that dog outside."

The police asked her if Tom had paid for the meals. She said, "Yes."

Well, the policeman said, "My dog eats in the house. I can't see any problem."

So Tom and Jigs finished their meals together in the restaurant. Tom thought the world of his Jiggers, and Jigs thought the world of Tom and T-bones.

A dog that I owned, one of several, was named Smokey. He was a mix between a Labrador and Dingo and lived to be fifteen or sixteen years old. When I lived on Trout Creek, I ran cattle with Smokey who was always a good cow dog. I could send him two-thirds of a mile across the place, and he'd bring all the cows to the barn. He was kind with children and every human bein'. Smokey was to me what Jigs was to Tom.

I had a royal family of dogs once that we called Queen, King, and Penny. Queen was a big German Shepherd. King was a little poodle and Penny was a Cocker Spaniel. All I can say about these dogs that I had at different times was I had a strong bond with all of them. Yes, I loved them and they loved me. Dogs are loyal and royal friends, sometimes more than people.

Another story I love about animals was one from Pete Bobalink, the character I already told you a little about and there's more to tell later. Anyway, Pete went out huntin' and seen a coyote. He took a shot and missed. Then he told me with his wild accent, "I-a shot-a again-a and hit-a the same damn-a place-a." He was such a cute little guy. That story still makes me smile.

As much as a human can love an animal, animals can really hurt humans too. I'm against these silly cartoons that show a little kid huggin' a bear. No little kid needs to think they can hug a bear. I'll tell you my bear stories and there was never no huggin' 'em.

I was walkin' up the street in Meeteetse, and Shank Maddox hollered at me. He said, "You want to go for a ride with me?"

I said, "Sure."

I went 'cuz anything that looked like a dollar in them days, you'd better jump at.

Shank said, "I got a sick bull up on Greybull Meadows and I'd like you to come help me doctor him."

We rode our horses up to Greybull Meadows, about 25-30 miles west of Meeteetse in the mountains. Sure enough, we found the bull with a slice about a foot and a half long on his shoulder, all swelled up with maggots rollin' out of the wound onto the ground. I didn't even have to rope him; all I did was get him by the horns. The poor old animal didn't even try to get away 'cuz he knew he was on the way out. We poured iodine and saltwater on the wound. Then the maggots really flooded to the ground.

Shanks said, "If I had my gun, I'd shoot him."

Neither one of us had a gun that day, so we continued on to a cabin and stayed there overnight. The next morning, we went to see how the bull was doin'. Shanks said on the way out, "I hope he's dead."

But sure enough, there stood that bull lookin' a tiny bit better. We glanced over and saw something black that we thought was a black calf so we rode over to investigate. Here, it was a black bear, dead and all swelled up. We knew right then what tore that bull's shoulder open.

We went back to the bull and did the same treatment—iodine and saltwater before we headed back down to Meeteetse.

Later, I met Shanks in Cody. He said, "Hey, Pete."

I stopped.

He continued, "You won't believe this, but I'm gonna tell you. The other day, there was a bull comin' down my road limpin'. Guess what? It was that bull we doctored up in Greybull Meadows. Can you believe that bull made it?"

I can't imagine the fight that bull and black bear went through, but the bull won in the long run. That bull was a registered Hereford.

In them days we didn't have Angus. The people Shanks cowboyed for, the Websters, used him for a ranch bull and got lots of babies out of him, but that bull never went back up on the mountain again.

Uncle Bob, Uncle Jack and my Granddad were out ridin' around the Fenton place one day when they spotted a dead cow. They rode to take a look at it and saw it had been killed by a bear 'cuz it had been dragged for several feet. They looked around and tracked where the bear had gone up a washout and dug a hole. A washout is where water comes streamin' hard and fast down a hill and washes a gully out on its way. The men decided they were gonna get that bear for killin' a cow, so they pulled sagebrush and threw it down in front of that hole and set it afire to smoke him out. It worked.

That bear came out and Uncle Jack shot him. The bear fell and his head landed in the fire. They got him out of the fire and skinned him. Later, they tanned the hide that made a huge rug. Us kids used to measure that rug. It was eleven feet from tail to where the neck was burned. That was a big bear—grizzly.

Another bear story happened when I was packin' horses for a sheep and cow outfit up on Dead Indian Mountain, north of Cody. That's beautiful country and ranchers ran a lot of their cows up there. Well, another cow was killed. I told my boss, and in turn, he told the Forest Service, who then told the forest ranger. The ranger finally came up on the mountain to see if he could find the bear that killed the cow. He had no trouble.

The bear came out of the woods. But, this time, that grizzly was with a bunch of other grizzlies. The ranger shot seven grizzlies dead that day. You know somethin'? He'd shoot one bear and another would jump right on top of the dropped bear. I don't know what was the matter with those bears. They'd just go after a dead one, time and time again. There sure was a lot of grizzlies in them days and they were big--real big. So, the people always shot them on sight.

A man I used to pack for was named Mr. Heald, ranched up on Skull Creek, who once told me, "Now, young man, you're gonna be packin' for me, and I wanna tell you what to do. When you go packin' into Butter Bowl Basin, don't tie those horses' tails tail-to-tail 'cuz

I lost six head of horses and a saddle horse that went over the cliff at least two hundred or three hundred feet down. It was a long ways down. Always turn your horses loose and walk behind them when you go down that narrow trail. If one horse gets spooked on that narrow trail, the whole string can go down. I'd rather lose the horses than you.

"Now, remember, when you look down that cliff, it's gonna be ghastly. It'll even make you think, 'Why would anyone ride a horse over that trail?' But just keep on comin'."

Well, turns out the guy that was packin' those horses jumped off his horse and ran back up the trail. Lo and behold, he ran right into, face-to-face, a big grizzly bear. He sure high-tailed it then up a little ravine. When the bear came by, the man said he could hear the bear claws clicking on the rocks. The bear knew the guy was there 'cuz he looked at him, sneered a little, but went right on by.

The horses were freakin' out 'cuz they smelled the bear and it cost them their lives. Lucky, it didn't cost that guy his life too. He was smart and dumb at the same time. Kinda like me all the time. If he'd been at the rear of the line of horses, he could have been knocked off the cliff too. Man, he was shit-house lucky.

While I was still a young man, there were people in Meeteetse who raised elk. They thought they'd make good money since elk were easy to domesticate 'cuz all you had to do was put a fence around them and let them eat. One of the elk ranchers was a family named Wilsons. Seems one day, the parents and some of the kids went into town while one Wilson boy stayed at home to keep an eye on things. When the rest of the family arrived back home, the boy was nowhere to be found.

They looked out in the pasture and saw an elk with the boy's shirt on its horns. That must have been awful. To think an elk could kill a boy was enough for the Wilsons who, after a while, ran all the elk off their place.

Another boy was killed too. This happened up on Paint Creek outside Cody to a family named Stenson who raised pigs. It seems like I'm just repeatin' myself, but this is what the newspaper, *The Cody Enterprise,* reported, and I read it.

The family went into Red Lodge to get supplies and left one boy at home. When they got back home, the boy wasn't around, so they started lookin' for him. Sure enough, they finally found him or parts of him. One of the boy's legs was stuck in the rails of the pig pen. He evidently fell into the pigpen and the pigs ate all of him except for that one leg. What an awful thing to happen.

Years later, my wife, my youngest son, and I lived outside Fort Washakie up Trout Creek Road on the Wind River Indian Reservation. It was here that I met a local fellow who brought an elk to be processed at the meat plant I ran with Doris. I processed the elk like the man wanted, but he didn't pay me money.

We traded for a mama bobcat that he had caught. Evidently, she was already bred since she gave us a kitten that spring. I built a pen for the mama and baby that was about 20 x 20 feet so they could get some good exercise. It was enclosed with chain-link fence on the top and all sides with a small gate. I fed them scraps from the meat plant that was like the food they would get in the wild. I never fed them anything else but always gave them plenty of water too.

The little kitten we named Pinky. Doris and I could handle her like she was a housecat. She was so beautiful and sweet. We'd take her into our house, and she loved it. Pinky was always careful too. If she'd climb around Doris' knickknacks on a shelf, she never turned one over.

We also had a bob-tailed housecat we called Mama Cat that more or less adopted Pinky. Both those cats would follow me to the garden, about two hundred yards away from the house and the bobcat pen. Pinky would get lost in the grass, and the first sound she'd make sounded just like she was sayin', "Pinky," so, logically, that became her name.

It was comical to hear a bobcat say, "Pinky," and when Mama Cat would hear the commotion, she'd come runnin' to see what Pinky and I was up to. The funniest thing to see was when Mama Cat would grab Pinky in her mouth, like mother cats do with their kittens, and walk all the way back to the house. Pinky was bigger than Mama Cat, so it was funnier than hell to see her try to walk that way. It looked like one big fuzz ball headin' to the house.

It was because of the mama bobcat and Pinky that I got into the bobcat business. Over six or seven years, I raised at least ten to fifteen bobcats living in that pen 'cuz I had divided the big pen into smaller pens. I never killed one for its pelt, but I sold them to two different parties when Doris and I moved from Trout Creek. I really liked those wildcats. I just didn't have the heart to kill any of them.

I didn't have the heart to let some baby bunnies die either. It was five or six years ago when I found five baby bunnies with their mom livin' in the manure pile by my house on Boulder Flats. Pretty soon, I found the mom dead on the highway. That highway has taken a lot of my animal friends. I hate that road. Anyway, I decided I'd try to save those baby bunnies.

They were only about two weeks old, just startin' to get fur on 'em. They were still curled up in the manure pile, waitin' for their mom to come back. I knew she wasn't comin' back, so I took those bunnies and the nest the mom had made and put them all in a shoe box. Then I put the shoe box in a spare bathtub to take care of them and keep 'em safe.

I fed 'em twice every day with an old baby bobcat nipple and bottle full of Carnation milk. They liked that milk and so do I. The only way I could tell if each one had gotten something to eat was by markin' them with colored markers. One was red, another blue, another green, yellow, and black. Each time I fed them, I'd take them out of one box and put them in another after their meal, and I'd put a mark on their little heads to be sure each one got their share.

Those little stinkers, they each got their share alright. Every one of them lived and when they grew up I'd sit out on my porch and throw 'em apples and apple peels. When they were about half-grown, they'd all line up to get their treats and I used those marks to be sure they were still OK. Sometimes, they'd fight over the peels or treats but they always came back. I still see one, to this very day, who stops in and checks to see if there are any apple scraps by the porch. She comes out and eats right now. Those were cute little rascals. They sure was.

One of my adventures as a young boy growing up around Meeteetse and Cody happened on the Greybull River. I went over to the Fenton place to visit my relatives and Uncle Bob. Us kids had herded up about 400-450 geese from down river, about six or seven miles from the first homestead. Uncle Bob sold the geese to some people from Billings, Montana, who wanted the down for pillows and mattresses.

Over four hundred blue-colored geese that were at least two feet tall were sold and butchered right there on the place. The people put the feathers in sacks and Uncle Bob burned the carcasses after they left. But to start, it was the kids' job to herd the geese from up the river too. So, we walked along the bank of the river, in the shallow parts, to move the geese down to the Fenton place. They were easy to move 'cuz they didn't fly, but they could sure duck under the water easy. If they did that, they could swim away from us. I remember Uncle Bob gave each of us a quarter a piece for herdin' those geese. He never did tell us what he got for him, but knowin' him, I'm sure he did fine. We were happy with a quarter since we thought we could buy all of the northern part of Wyoming with it if we wanted to.

I'm gonna tell you a little joke to end the animal section of these stories. Some of you might find it spicy or offensive. I think it's funny. There was a man and his girlfriend who decided to have a picnic. While they were drivin' out to the picnic grounds, the man said, "Do you see all those horses? They're all mine."

They drove on a little farther, and the man said, "Do you see all those cattle? Well, I'm not much of a hand to brag, but they're all mine."

Then they drove further, and the man said, "You see all those sheep? I'm not braggin', but those sheep are all mine."

As they drove on a little further, they came to a bridge where a little boy was fishin'. The man thought he'd impress his girlfriend, so he talked to the boy. He asked the little boy, "Are you catchin' any fish?"

The little boy answered, "Yeah, some about the size of your peter."

The man put the old car in gear and headed off that bridge 'cuz the boy had embarrassed him. While they were eatin' their lunch, the man looked at his girlfriend and said, "I'm not much of a hand to brag, but that boy is catchin' some pretty good-sized fish."

Lundie and Partner, c. 2017, *(Karen King photo)*

Lundie and Pinky, the bobcat, c. 1977, *(Thayer family photo)*

Lundie and Pinky c. 1980, *(Thayer family photo)*

Lundie feeding Pinky, c. 1976, *(Thayer family photo)*

Pinky, c. 1978, *(Thayer family photo)*

Lundie feeding a bum calf in his living room, c. 1982, *(Thayer family photo)*

Lundie loving his favorite steer, c. 1984, *(Thayer family photo)*

Lundie on Rocky, c. 1986, *(Thayer family photo)*

CHAPTER 3

Weather

When I was a boy of about twelve years old, we lived in Cody durin' the brutal cold winter of 1927. One day, my hero, my big brother Bugs, asked me if I wanted to go for a ride for a couple of days. I jumped at the chance.

Bugs said, "We're gonna go gather up those saddle horses that left the place last fall. We need to get some feed in 'em."

I said, "OK, let's go."

Bugs got on a buckskin saddle horse and I was ridin' Amel, a bay. He thought the other saddle horses were runnin' up on Carter Mountain, so we intended to stay the night 'cuz it was fifteen to 20 miles from home and we knew we couldn't drive them all home before dark. It was one of the worst decisions we ever made. The weather turned so bad we regretted it by late afternoon when we came on the herd of saddle horses at the foot of Carter Mountain. We pushed 'em a little ways toward home before it got dark on us. We had to stay overnight for sure then.

Bugs said, "We'll stay overnight at the Old Sawmill and pack the horses up in the morning."

We picketed our horses and Bugs and I walked over to the Old Sawmill. There were cracks through it so bad you could have thrown your hat through it any place, but we decided it was better to sleep there than out on the ground since the weather had turned so blasted cold. The temperature was so low that when Bugs breathed, his whiskers turned white with icicles.

Bugs told me to stay awake until midnight and then he'd take over the watch. I agreed to this arrangement. He insisted again that I stay awake. I told him I would, but bein' a kid, I got sleepy and decided to take just a little snooze. Thank God, Bugs stayed awake and caught me snoozin'. He ruffled and roughed me up good to wake me up.

After that, we both ended up stayin' awake all the rest of that night. Bugs saved my life since I didn't know what I was doin'. I know I would have froze to death if I'd gone to sleep or been without my big brother. Today, they call it hypothermia. Back then, we called it goddamned cold. We made it through the night, which was the worse night I've ever put in. The wind blowin' through the cracks in that old sawmill and us tryin' to keep warm was hopeless, but we made it through somehow. That was the first night of the famous blizzard of 1927.

The next morning, we got up, gathered our horses real early, and started to go after the other horses. That's when I learnt another lesson. I started to put the bit in Amel's mouth when my big brother roughed me up again.

He said, "You don't go to work and put a cold bit in a horse's mouth. You have to warm it up for him."

I said, "How do I warm it up? I don't have any fire or anything and I'm nearly froze myself."

He said, "Put it between your legs or under your arms for a few minutes. Then put it in his mouth."

The lessons from Bugs go on and on like when I was gonna put the saddle blanket on Amel. The sweat from the ride the day before had frozen and I was going to put the frozen side right next to Amel's back. Bugs stopped me again.

He said, "What the hell ya' doin'? Turn that saddle blanket over. You don't want to put that frozen blanket next to his hide."

I did what my big brother said.

We finally got mounted up and took off ridin'. Within about a half a mile, we came to a rancher's house with smoke comin' from the chimney. That was a most wonderful sight, for sure, since it was so bitter cold. We rode down to the place and Bugs asked the rancher if we could come in and warm up a bit.

The rancher said, "Sure. Come on in. What the hell are you doin' out here this early on such a cold mornin'?"

Bugs said, "We slept the night over the hill in the Old Sawmill."

The rancher said, "I can't believe it. Before I'd get that goddamned cold, I would have burned down the sawmill."

After we warmed up some, his wife fed us a wonderful breakfast. We thanked them lots before we mounted up again.

In a short distance, we picked up the herd and drove 'em to what was called the Green Wall Corrals which was located on upper Sulphur Creek. You can't believe what we saw. Two spiked elk went right in the corral along with the horses we were drivin'. We finally got the elk out and cut the strays out from our string so we had all our horses ready to head home, but Old Buckskin and Amel were played out. They had put in a hard ride in that cold weather.

Bugs said to me, "I'll ride the sorrel mare. Do you think you can ride her colt home?"

Me, bein' real young, said, "I'll try."

Bugs said, "I'll snub him up to my saddle horn and you get on him."

Bugs saddled and bridled the colt and I got on. Believe it or not, after a couple of times around that corral, all snubbed up tight, that colt didn't try anything. He was cold broke, so to say. So Bugs unsnubbed him and let him stand there with the saddle and bridle.

We were awful hungry, horses and humans. All of us were gettin' weaker by the minute and the temperature never went up, only down.

Bugs said, "If you spot a cottontail, let me know."

Sure enough, I went over to open the corral gate and right there was a cottontail. Bugs was an expert shot and when I pointed my finger toward the rabbit, Bugs pulled his .45 revolver out and shot. The bullet never hit the rabbit but was close enough to daze him. Bugs just walked over and put one foot on the rabbit's head and pulled him by the hind feet. Sure enough, the head came right off.

Bugs said, "We can't eat him raw. We're gonna have to cook him. You look around and find somethin' to cook him in."

Well, I looked and found an old piss-pot someone had used as an indoor toilet. The piss-pot was half full of sand that the wind had blown in and it was all frozen with the new snow. I sat it on the fire that Bugs started so we could cook our rabbit. Pretty soon, the sand and snow had melted and Bugs told me, "Go over to the creek and wash it out real good. I mean real good."

I tried my best to get it clean since I knew what it had been used for. I took sand and creek water and scrubbed hard, the best I could before takin' it back to the fire. We put the rabbit in, boiled him and really enjoyed the meal. We were both starvin' since we hadn't eaten in more than two days, since the rancher's wife had fixed us breakfast. Boy, that was a good rabbit, and that's all it tasted of, nothin' shitty.

After about two weeks, Bugs asked me if I could still taste that yummy rabbit.

I said, "Yes."

He said, "I can too. I don't know if it was the rabbit's flavor or the pot."

We both had been burpin' for prittin' near two weeks and every time we did, it tasted like that rabbit or the pot. I don't know 'til this day which one.

Anyway, Bugs got on the sorrel mare about dark and I got on the colt. We headed out and it got even colder than it had been when we froze up on Carter Mountain, but we headed home. That colt just followed his mom like he was brand new and here he was a three-year-old. We're lucky he was so good.

About 2:30 the next morning, we finally got back home. To greet us, was Amel and the buckskin that beat us home. They were both standin' at the gate. When I opened the gate, they came in with us. That's the first time Hell's Bells was ever ridden. As I mentioned previously, Hell's Bells left me later in the dirt at the new Cody Airport, but on that trip he was a real champ.

During this same time, around 1927 in the same damned winter, we got a bigger blizzard. I remember well that we had a line strung from the house to the outhouse and put a bell at each end. When you got your job done in the outhouse, you'd ring the bell to let them know you were headin' for the house. When you went to the outhouse, you'd ring the bell to let people know you were headin' out. That system really helped us all and could have saved our lives since many of my brothers and sisters were still little and they needed to go too. Mama made sure the line and bells were workin' to save her kids.

That storm was so bad that cattle and horses froze to death standin' up or lyin' down, but none of us died even though other people around Park County died especially the sheepherders. Can you imagine those poor old sheepherders livin' in camps with only a canvas over the top of them in weather like that? They were strong men. For every one that died, there was a hundred that lived.

Now, Wyoming had lots of blizzards and cold temperatures. The winter of 1930 was really cold with lots of snow too. The Cody School was closed a lot that winter. In 1939, it was even colder but hardly any snow. Just cold wind followed by colder wind, dry and cold. In 1941, I was in the army when the Japs hit Pearl Harbor, but there was lots of snow in Wyoming then too.

During each of these winters, the livestock and wildlife had it really rough. In 1927, lots of cattle and horses froze to death. Even a few sheep died. The only animals that came out OK were down on the rivers among the cottonwood trees and willows. Even some of them didn't make it.

One of hardest winters ever in Wyoming was the winter of 1948–49. All of Wyoming was snowed in for days at a time. The trains goin' along the southern part, between Rock Springs and Rawlins, were all snowbound. My brother, Sid, lived near Rawlins and he told me there were four passenger trains stranded outside Rawlins that winter.

Sid's house was down in a dip, protected some from the Rawlins' wind, but there was no good shelter anywhere that winter. The wind drifted the snow right over the top of their house, and the only way they could get in or out was by cuttin' a hole in the ceilin' and goin' out through the roof.

Another instance of how bad that storm was when Sid and Carl tried to save some sheep. A man asked them if they would help him get feed to his sheep. Sid took two horses, one he was ridin' and the other a packhorse, and he and Carl rode into that band of sheep. On the pack saddle were two bales of hay that they scattered a little at a time along the trail they made goin' in and out. Those sheep followed that little bit of hay all the way back to the ranch. This helped save prittin' near 1,000 sheep, but a few head of sheep suffocated in the snow 'cuz it was that deep.

As a gesture of appreciation, the sheep man told Sid and Carl that he'd give them the suffocated sheep's skins if they'd skin them. Well, that seemed like a pretty good deal, so Sid and Carl started skinnin'. They got the job done and headed back to Rawlins when they got their truck stuck in the snow. They only had a little gas and it was already dark as hell.

They decided to crawl under some of the sheep hides to sleep that night. Well, the hides were green and they froze solid, stiff, on top of my brothers. It was a miracle they didn't suffocate themselves that night. They had to cut their way out from under those frozen sheep hides to get the truck runnin' toward home. Then they had to shovel for hours to get the truck unstuck. Just as they pulled into Sid's place, they ran out of gas, only a little bit away. That was a miracle too.

When Doris, the kids, and I lived in St. Helens, it snowed and rained a lot in 1956. When it finally thawed out, the Columbia River flooded and the paper mill where I worked had to shut down. The insulation factory closed too. Another sawmill, Pulp and Talbot, shut down too. In fact, everything that was built along the river had to be closed 'cuz the water kept gettin' higher. Durin' that flood, everything was shut down for about two weeks before we could get back to work. The Columbia River near St. Helens is usually about three hundred to four hundred yards wide; it varies. But in 1956, that river was at least three-quarters of mile across and carryin' billions of gallons of water.

My father-in-law said, "No one can build a dam that will hold that water."

It was so bad even the big ships couldn't move and log rafts broke loose with loads of lumber floodin' down river. There were no lives lost, that I know of 'cuz there was plenty of warnin' from the port authorities who had reports of the river crossin' over the tops of all the dams on the whole Columbia River. Even Grand Coulee had to release their water 'cuz they were afraid it would flood the whole valley which would leave lots of people dead.

When my family moved from Oregon to Fremont County, Wyoming, in 1963, it wasn't a picnic either. A lot of snow and cold weather that winter hit us on the place we owned up North Fork at Fort Washakie. The snow was so deep that year I had to take the tractor and the ditcher to clear paths so the cows could eat their hay. Cows can't dig through snow like horses can, so if you want your herd to live in a winter like that, you have to feed 'em everyday. I had to use the tractor every mornin' and every afternoon to take my kids to or from the school bus. It was surprisin' that Fort Washakie School stayed open so much that year since it was really rough.

Now days, the weather in Wyoming can get plumb hot. But, we just carried on with our lives doin' what we had to do. When the Dust Bowl hit in the 1930s about the same time as the national Depression, Wyoming didn't get hit as bad as other places by the dust, but we suffered a lot with the Depression and it got awful hot in Wyoming. We didn't even notice that other states like Texas, Oklahoma, Arkansas, and Nebraska all through that area were in such terrible conditions.

People by the millions migrated from all over to California to get out of the dust. The dust got in people's lungs, especially old people and young kids. They called it dust pneumonia and lots of folks died. Actually, they suffocated.

I remember another storm we called the Columbus Day windstorm, around 1957 or 1958. It came in at Santa Rosa, California, and hit all the way up to Washington State where Doris and I lived with our family in St. Helens. The storm went back out to sea in Oceanside, Washington. Later, I saw an aerial picture of the storm and it looked like a great big mowin' machine had been through that area. It cut a wide swath about three-quarters of a mile wide for approximately eight hundred to nine hundred miles before it went back out to sea.

I lost heavy in that storm. It knocked my apple trees over and blew my great big barn over that had about 60 tons of hay in the hayloft. When the barn fell, it killed one milk cow. I had a registered purebred Hereford bull in the barn named Rollo. Believe it or not, all that hay and barn fell right on top of old Rollo but never hurt him one bit. He was lying right between two strong joists and lived. The only injury he had was a big sliver that ran under the hide on his back. I knew he was under the hay, so I worked until I was black in the face, trying to get Rollo out.

Have you ever worked so hard and you're so tired that your eyesight turns blurry and everything looks black? Well, that's how hard I worked to get my bull out—black in the face. I couldn't get him out that night, but I figured he was hungry, so I brought him some apples. That bull ate those apples right out of my hands. The next morning, I can't understand this either, but I took my chainsaw to where the barn used to stand and cut those joists from around Rollo. It took Rollo about an hour to find his feet. When he got up, he walked right across what was left of the hayloft floor that had fallen.

Why I didn't set that hay afire with that chainsaw, I do not know. I kept Rollo for five or six years and got all kinds of calves out him. Old Rollo was probably the only good thing that came out of that Columbus Day windstorm.

That wind blew my garage and my chicken coop over and the only thing I had left standing was the brand new home that I'd just built. My children and wife were in the house the whole time where I had them stand under a beam that was braced real good. The wind was so strong that a big plate glass window in our dinin' room just bowed out well beyond its casin' but didn't break. It would just go in and out like someone breathin'. I lost some of the sidin' off the new house and all of the shingled roof. We were so lucky 'cuz several people died in that storm. I got 30 days unpaid leave off from my job at the paper mill, if you want to call it "off," 'cuz I worked my ass off tryin' to get that hay under a roof of some kind and get the house re-shingled. Luckily, it didn't rain. I managed to save all the hay, get the house re-roofed, and then went back to work at the paper mill. Three or four days after that, it rained buckets and never stopped until spring. That's the God's truth. I was luckier than hell on savin' that hay and that house. The good Lord held me by the hand since the house was brand new and it would have been ruined if the rain hit it before the roof was on. Phew, I got the new roof on just in time.

I was lucky to have some good helpers too. I hired a boy called Warner and my wife and son did wonders. They pulled all the nails from the used barn wood and stacked it in piles so I could use it again. I didn't have to buy much new wood 'cuz Warner, my son, and Doris did such good work.

Now, Wyoming is famous for its winds. We had plenty all my life, but it was somethin' you just got used to. The other night, it blew hard again, but it wasn't anythin' new. Some people say the wind made old timers crazy 'cuz it blew so often and so hard. If that's the case, I shoulda been an idiot all my life and never lived this long. I've seen a lot of Wyoming wind and I'm still here.

Trout Creek, spring 2017, Greyhound and horses. *(Karen King photo)*

North of Meeteetse, summer 2016. *(Karen King photo)*

Trout Creek Wyoming, winter. 2013 *(Karen King photo)*

Trout Creek Wyoming, summer 2014 *(Karen King photo)*

CHAPTER 4

Military

I was in the military, but they're not very happy times. It started when a friend and I met in Cody. He told me he had an idea of where we could get a regular supply of Bull Durham, a tobacco we rolled up and smoked. He said we wouldn't have to bum one another for a cigarette anymore.

I said, "How?"

He said, "We can join the National Guard. They'll pay us $1 a month if we show up for drills once a month."

I asked, "That's all we do?"

He said, "Yep."

So we did it and that was the beginning of my military career. All for smokin' Bull Durham and thinkin' we were big shots.

Anyway, we became guardsmen in Cody. Everything went fine for a while until Uncle Sam decided we were gonna be soldiers. That same uncle inducted us into federal service. All of the Wyoming National Guard was inducted. By the time my hitch was over, I had landed in Headquarters and Service Troop which worked together in the 115th Cavalry. We supplied A, B, C, D, E, and F Troops, our regiment, with groceries, coal, uniforms, boots, guns, and ammunition. We delivered anything else they needed when they ordered it and got approval from the quarter master.

To start my hitch, we were ordered to meet at 8:00 a.m. at the Irma Hotel downtown. I lived in Cody at the time, but when I was ready to go to the Irma, I discovered it had snowed about three feet the night before. I rode Baldy down to the Keystone Barn which was a livery stable right downtown about one block from the Irma. I tied him up there and then walked to the Irma. Everyone there said that we weren't gonna leave that day 'cuz of the snow. Boy, was everyone wrong.

Here came two big rotary snowplows that cleared the way for big Greyhound buses to follow through the snow. The buses turned and parked right in front of the Irma. About 20 of us young men from Park County loaded up in one of the buses. In the other buses were young men they'd picked up from different towns since they started in Montana and stopped in Powell before makin' it to Cody. We were headed next to Greybull, Basin, Worland, and Thermopolis. We were in the army, then, for sure.

The merchants in Cody were really nice to us. They gave me three quarts of whiskey, four cartons of cigarettes, cookies, and candy just like they did for every man on that bus. When we stopped at other towns, those merchants gave their boys treats too. We were all well-healed, which means we were ready to go. Boy, were we ready when we left Cody, but the snow kept a-comin'. The snow never let up until we got to Douglas and then it started to peter out some.

Since neither my buddy or me drank, it was a rough ride for us 'cuz most of the other men were getting' pie-eyed. We sat in the very last seat at the back of the bus where two other men beside us were so drunk they passed out. My buddy and I pushed 'em down on the floor and used 'em for footrests all the way to Cheyenne. Turned out they were good for somethin'.

Boy, oh boy, was that Greyhound bus a mess when we got to Cheyenne. I was glad when I finally got off to breathe fresh air. I sent my civilian clothes back home through the post office at Fort Frances E. Warren and my whiskey too. It was more medicine for my family if they needed it. I wasn't gonna use it then and still don't today.

After I got my final health exam, I was officially in the army and we left Cheyenne. From Cheyenne, they sent us on a train to Fort Leavenworth, Kansas, that took at least one full day. In Leavenworth, we took our basic training for about six weeks. From Kansas, we went on another train, west this time, which took about three days to Fort Lewis, Washington. By the time those trains pulled in from Leavenworth, there were about 2,800 troopers on them. The reason it took so long to get anywhere is 'cuz they would unload all the men to have us exercise some. We'd have to do the regular army exercises like push-ups, runnin', walkin', and jumpin'—anything that would make us move.

In Fort Lewis, the 115th Cavalry Recon Regiment was in the regular army. Every man who had been on those trains was now in the 115th. A recognizance unit would scope out the enemy—where it was camped, how many soldiers were there, and where their guns was placed. It's a very important unit in any war. While at Fort Lewis, all 2,800 of us heard about the Japs hittin' Pearl Harbor on December 7, 1941, which really changed the 115th Calvary Recon. Since we were recognizance, we more or less got scattered all over the Pacific coast. After Pearl Harbor was hit, it took us about fifteen or 20 days to regroup. Men from all over back east were bein' shipped to the west coast in case the Japs came on shore. It was a big part of recon units' jobs—to be sure the Japs weren't comin' any closer to American soil.

I can't tell you everything that happened from then on. But one day, I landed on top of the Manegan Hospital in Fort Lewis in charge of a .50 caliber machine gun nest with three other machine gun operators. I set up a cross-fire nest on that roof with one machine gun in each corner.

The officer in charge said, "Any airplane that comes close to this hospital, shoot that son-of- a-bitch down. All our pilots have orders not to fly over this hospital."

Before he walked away, he pointed at me and said, "You're in charge."

That's why I set up the cross fire with men and guns that could shoot down a plane from any direction. The God's truth is I wanted to shoot at a plane 'cuz I was an expert .50 caliber machine gun operator and so were the other three men. I would have shot any plane down 'cuz you didn't have time to see whatever symbol it was flyin' and I had to follow orders.

I was so proud on the roof of that hospital to see all the men and ladies who came there to join the army. Young and old, and even WWI veterans enlisted. I knew why I was there, for sure. The Japs had killed so many of our young soldiers, we weren't going to let them kill any more.

In a few days, I was ordered to report to Gray's Field in Fort Lewis, Washington, which was an airport with a real landing strip not like the one at Cody. The camp at Fort Lewis was huge. We had a hospital, an airport, barracks, and mess halls enough for thousands of men. I can't tell you exactly how many of us were there, but there was more than ten thousand, I'd guess. Hell's fire, we had 2,800 ourselves with every kind of soldier there too. Artillery, Infantry, and the 98th was there with their 2,400 mules. We'd have had our horses there too, but after Pearl Harbor, we became mechanized with tanks, scout cars, jeeps, and command cars. We had prittin' near every vehicle you can think of but no horses.

Fort Lewis was the command headquarters and we had a very nice parade and trainin' field too. It was sure lots better than at Leavenworth. The whole camp was surrounded by majestic fir trees that made the camp more attractive than most military bases too. While I was stationed at Fort Lewis, a beautiful lady came into my life too—Doris.

I got the first airplane ride of my life from Gray's Field in Fort Lewis, Washington, to San Francisco, California. That was the first time I ever rode up in the air in a plane instead of off a horse. It was a small plane with probably fourteen to sixteen men onboard besides the pilot and copilot.

In San Francisco, I was assigned to a half-track which is a vehicle that has tracks on the back end and regular truck tires on the front. The whole thing was made out of armor plate. I rode that half-track as a .50 caliber machine gunner and proceeded to round up Japs in the San Francisco area, whether dead or alive. We went from countryside to right downtown San Francisco's Chinatown. We picked up live Japanese people and put 'em on army trucks and then delivered 'em to Frisco where we turned 'em over to an army unit that was in charge of evacuation. That army unit was in a huge building right down by the railroad tracks. From there, I was told they were sent to "concentration camps" like the one outside Cody that was called Heart Mountain.

I also saw some dead ones. The officer in charge of us called our vehicle the "gut wagon." He was kind of a smart-ass 'cuz he wasn't pickin' up his own guts. If we saw some dead people, our officer would call another unit that took care of the dead. I was told that the corpses were taken to an incinerator and disposed of that way. I had to go to an old farmhouse once and found seven dead Japanese there—grandparents to babies. An officer then told me that he thought they may have killed themselves, but I don't think anyone found out for sure.

It was a tough time 'cuz those Japanese were Americans too and didn't want to leave their homes and I didn't want to either since I was satisfied with the National Guard back in good ole Wyoming. Anyway, lots of Americans who lost their boys in Pearl Harbor took revenge on lots of Asian people who were killed not just by white people but also by the Chinese who hated the Japs too. They killed a lot in Chinatown and other places all along the west coast.

My detail lasted about four days and then the 115th Cavalry was split up. Each troop was sent to different parts of California, Washington, and Oregon on patrol. Our troop was stationed in Salem, Oregon, where we patrolled from Seaside to Newport, Oregon. That was over 110 miles, I think, and we went on different routes that weren't straight routes. Then we regrouped as a full regiment at Fort Lewis again for a while before we got orders to pack up the whole outfit and load up on another train that took us south to San Diego, California.

It was there, the army split the 115th right down the middle. We became trainin' catteries, in army lingo. I stayed with the 115th, while the other half went to the 126th. Our jobs were to train draftees. I was in the armored unit for Headquarters and Service Units and trained draftees on guns, from machine guns to side arms.

The army was nuts, plumb nuts, by sendin' us here, there, and everywhere. From San Diego, we regrouped again, and they sent the 115th and the 126th to Camp Polk, Louisiana. I got orders to go from Louisiana back to Fort Leavenworth. It wasn't just me that got those orders but about two hundred of us men. While I was at Camp Polk, I got different orders. The army at that time, counted the time we had served in the National Guard and Federal Army Service and said they would discharge us on points, which meant we'd been in the military for over four years already and it was time to be discharged. In Leavenworth, I got my discharge papers and headed back to Cody to see my folks before I went back to join my wife in St. Helens, Oregon.

Before I was discharged, I met some pretty interestin' people in the army. I was assigned to a mail truck delivery job in the army and they also assigned a gunner to go with me just to deliver mail. My gunner was a half-assed alcoholic named Shorty Gilbert whose rifle was bigger than he was. The reason they assigned him to me was 'cuz they knew I never drank and they thought I might be able to help him. Shorty always wanted me to stop on our route to get a beer, but I never would.

One day, I asked Shorty, "Do you want a beer?"

His eyes lit up like a Christmas tree and he quickly said, "Yes!"

I told him to stay in the vehicle and watch the mail and I'd go in to get us a couple. I went into a place and bought us two root beers, one for him and one for me. He looked at the root beer like I'd shot him in the guts and he wouldn't drink a drop of it. So I did. I drank both of 'em.

He was mad and about half-pissed when he said, "I'm gonna get off this rig when I get back to Fort Lewis."

He told the officer what I'd done, but they wouldn't move him anywhere else except with me. He was my mascot.

Another incident happened when we were drivin' on the outside of Seattle and passed a big, beautiful, red brick building every time we delivered mail. We always wondered what the hell was in there. We had a little time one day and we decided to drive into that building and find out. Shorty, the driver, was real short and when we met a big, tall man near the entrance, Shorty got lots shorter.

Lo, and behold, Shorty asked him, "What's cookin', Doc?"

This tall guy looked down at him with a kind of frown before he broke out laughin'. Neither Shorty or me knew what the building was for, so he asked the tall guy if he knew. He knew alright. That building was a crematorium which was why the big guy laughed when Shorty asked what was cookin'.

The tall guy took us on a little tour of that beautiful building which was full of big brass vases the Chinese used to hold the ashes of their loved ones. Some of them were really beautiful. I could go to that building right today and show you how out-of-this-world it was. All around this great big room were these vases behind glass that had been sold to people like the plots we have in big cemeteries. Those were very beautiful vases and some of them looked like gold.

I told you about ridin' trains in the army. There's a funny story about one train ride with my sister, Mary, and her daughter. I got a furlough while I was in California and I told Mary that I was gonna go back home to Wyoming. Boy, she wanted to go with me.

I went down to the depot and asked the station master if I could take Mary with me.

He automatically said, "Yes. Any serviceman can take his wife and family with him."

He never asked me if Mary was my wife, so I got a bright idea that Mary would tell him that she was my wife and her daughter, about three years old at the time, was our daughter. It sounded like a good plan.

The little girl was coached to call me "Daddy" not "Uncle Pepper" like she always had. She was a really good learner and we practiced a lot until we got to the depot to board the train. Well, the train didn't leave right away and "our" daughter got impatient.

Finally, she says to me, "Uncle Pepper, when are we leavin'?"

The station master looked at Mary and me with a crooked grin. My heart sank fast, but he just gave us a signal with his thumb to go ahead and get onboard. Phew, we were lucky. Mary would never have been able to leave California to go see the family durin' that war if she hadn't been with me. The little girl almost blew our cover, but the station master was good-hearted and knew we were pullin' shit over his eyes. But, he let it go.

That train was all military and that little girl was so cute—many soldiers hadn't seen anything that sweet in a long time. I can still see her singin', "Mares eat oats and does eat oats and little lambs eat ivy. A kid'll eat ivy too, wouldn't you?" That little three-year-old would dance and we all thought she was a good entertainer. Even though all those servicemen were hard up, they gave that little girl tips that amounted to $85 by the end of the trip. Mary didn't like it, but those soldiers also gave her sweets like Coca-Cola and candy that she had never tasted before 'cuz they were expensive.

Once, I delivered groceries to the Air Force and E Troop in Fort Lewis. Before I could unload the E Troop groceries, I had to move some horse meat that I was gonna deliver to the Air Force for their dogs. An E Troop trooper came by and he spotted the stamp on a side of meat that said, "Pure horse meat."

He asked me, "Have you been in this outfit long? How much horse meat have you eaten?"

I told him, "I eat it all the time," and then he shut up.

He told a lot of other troopers that they were all eatin' horse meat. That night, they had a beautiful steak meal with all the trimmin's, but not one of them would eat it. Bein' from Wyoming, we didn't eat horse meat but sure enjoyed a good steak. As I finished unloadin' E Troop's groceries, I realized there was sure a lot of dumb asses in the Army and Air Force.

When I was stationed in California, we were ordered to put on our side arms and keep them loaded. An officer said, "We're goin' out on patrol. There's a bunch of Mexicans from Old Mexico that are beatin' a lot of people to death with chains, includin' servicemen. If you run across any of these people, don't get close to them. If they give you any static, just shoot 'em."

It was our duty to protect servicemen and civilians whether it was from Japs or Mexicans. We were serious about our jobs too. I put my .45 revolver pistol on, which was standard issue for the cavalry's side arm and went to see my sister in Los Angeles. As I came down the street, I ran across about six of these illegal Mexicans from Old Mexico that the army called Zoot Suiters 'cuz they carried great big chains in their pockets. Those men gave me no static, but I sure kept my distance and then went on to see my sister.

Mary said she'd been holdin' her breath when she saw me comin' down the street by those people.

When she saw my pistol, she said, "Now, I see why you kept comin'. I'm glad it went well."

In the barracks at Fort Lewis, an officer came in and said, "You, you, you," pointin' to about ten of us. "Get your side arms on and come as you are," which meant in our fatigues.

We were loaded on an army truck headed for Tacoma, Washington, where we arrived at a great big four-story building and unloaded. The officer sent two men into the back of the building to secure it. He told the policeman who was there that he was relieved and that law enforcement was behind him.

Pretty soon, soldiers were sent to secure the front of the building. There were no doors or a way that we could see to get to the fourth story unless you went up a great big staircase that was outside. I was climbin' up that staircase when a thought crossed my mind. "I wonder what would happen if this building ever caught fire."

The officer wasn't very polite when we finally got to the fourth floor. He just raised his leg up and kicked the damn door down, and we walked in. There was a black man laid on the floor dead. Come to find out, the fourth floor was a black whorehouse, the whole floor.

A black woman was standin' over the black man with a knife in her hand and asked, "What are you whiteys doin' here?"

The officer said, "Us whiteys are here to secure this building until the black soldiers show up."

At that time, they had black MPs and white MPs, and they policed their own race. A little while later, two black MPs came up those steps and we went down 'em, headin' back to Fort Lewis.

One of the funniest guys I ever met in the army came from Rock Springs, Wyoming. His name was Johnny Rawlins and he knew Pete Bobalink who I had met when I was a kid. Well, Johnny could talk just exactly like Mr. Bobalink which really cheered me up. We decided we wanted to learn international Morse code while we were in the service, so Johnny and I were assigned to telegraph machines.

They'd put us on the Fort Lewis parade field in pup tents to practice our Morse code and test how fast we could get messages out. Everything was goin' fine, although I was a lot slower than Johnny in usin' the telegraph machine. We were in those hot little tents for hours. Johnny was in one tent and I was in another, so we would send each other messages back and forth. It was pretty good practice for both of us, except when Johnny decided to use Morse code and talk just like Mr. Bobalink over the telegraph. It really tickled me to get those messages in that accent. It was really fun for a while until we found out the officers were listenin' to us too.

Yep, the officer didn't think it was so funny when he'd hear our messages. He decided to chew me out and accuse me of talkin' that way. I wouldn't squeal on Johnny, even though the officer gave me a really bad time. I told the officer to shove the Morse code and the machine. I went back to my outfit.

Old Johnny became a really good Morse code operator. I think Johnny went with the 126th 'cuz I never saw him or used the Morse code with him again.

While I was stationed in Salem, a civilian asked if there were any Thayers in our unit. The officer brought him over to see me sayin', "This is Lundie Thayer from Cody, Wyoming."

The civilian's name was Mr. McCoy, whose dad was married to my dad's sister, but I'd never met him before. Come to find out, these McCoys developed the Blue Lake Bean that you find in any seed catalogue to this very day. He developed both the pole and bush bean. That night, they invited me for dinner at their home in Statton, Oregon. At that dinner table, there were Coast Guard, Navy, Marines, Army, and Air Force. And at that meal, every one of us was related somehow to the McCoys. It's really good that I have bean relatives 'cuz I sure have eaten a whole bunch of beans in my life and I grew a few. The military served us a lot of beans too.

Another time when I met the real McCoys, I visited their home in Statton and found Mr. McCoy with a bad hand. One of his short-horned bulls ran a horn clear through his palm. The bull wasn't being mean; it was just an accident since Mr. McCoy's hand was in the wrong place when the bull shook his head. Those McCoys had real pretty animals and really good beans.

I never went overseas with the military or with anyone even though I would have liked to. Two of my brothers went. Jerry went to the Pacific and Carl was in the European theatre. Every time I went to the port of embarkation, they'd turn me back to my unit. Why? Well, there was a military rule after three Sullivan brothers went down on one ship. I was told that I couldn't go overseas 'cuz I would have been the third Thayer boy posted off American soil.

December 1941 was the worst month I ever put in personally. Not only was Pearl Harbor attacked, but my Mama died too. While stationed at Fort Lewis, I got word she was in St. Vincent's Hospital in Billings, Montana, on her deathbed. I decided I had to go see her and told my captain that I was leavin'.

He said, "You can't. We need you bad."

I told him, "I'm leavin' anyway. I'm not the only damn soldier in this army."

He said, "I'll go see the colonel."

While he went to see the colonel, I put on my uniform and started to get ready to go back to Wyoming.

Pretty soon, the captain showed up again and said, "Do you have any money?"

I told him the truth, "I have none. I'm plannin' on hitchhikin'."

The captain said, "Wait a little while."

Sure enough, he was a great guy. While I waited, the captain went among the servicemen and officers to get donations to send me back to Wyoming to see my dyin' mama.

He said, "I'm going to give you a message from the colonel. He said that he lost his mother too and that he can't blame you for wantin' to go home. So he gave me $3 as a donation for you, Trooper, and asked if I would take up a collection amongst the other troopers, so you can go home. He also said to be sure to find someone to stand in for you at revelry while you're gone."

Sure enough, the captain collected $35 which was plenty of money to get me home. I took the money and went out on the highway since I'd told the Captain I was gonna take a chance thumbin' a ride. He told me to do whatever I had to. You can't believe this, but there was a whole bunch of guys hitchin' too. If there is a God, he was with me 'cuz the first big truck that came along stopped for me.

I got in and the driver asked me, "Where you headin', soldier?"

I told him I had to make it to Billings, Montana.

The driver said, "You're in luck. This truck will eventually get to Billings."

I stayed on that truck the whole day and night until we got to Butte, Montana, when the truck driver said that it was the end of the line for him. So we got out and he said, "Now, stay right here. I've got to go on into Butte, but there will be another driver comin' this way that will take this truck into Billings. When he gets here, he'll pick you up."

I rode with the second driver all the way to Billings. Both those drivers had bought me meals and everything I needed, so I still had lots of money in my pocket. Every penny of the donations the men at Fort Lewis had given me, I still had. I took a taxi to St. Vincent's Hospital in Billings, but that driver didn't charge me anything either.

When I went into the hospital, I met my brother, Bugs, in the lobby, and we went up to see Mama. She was seriously ill but raised up and said to me, "Pete, kill a goddamned Jap for me too."

That's the last time we spoke. We buried her December 23, 1941, in Cody. My brother Sid gave me $40, so I bought a bus ticket and made it back to my unit. It still brings a tear to my eye. She was a good woman.

Oh, for the love of Jimmy Rogers, I almost forgot. The only funny thing about December 1941 was at revelry. Sure enough, while I was gone, my unit covered for me at roll call time. Someone would answer when the name Thayer was called, "Here."

Well, the first day I got back, I went to revelry and said "Here" for myself along with two guys who were still coverin' for me.

The captain said, "You can sure stutter, Thayer," as we all laughed.

I paid the boys back includin' the colonel and the captain as best I could. Well, I'll say one thing—those boys from Wyoming, we stayed together. They were damned good boys too. We always helped someone get home if they needed to 'cuz our $21 a month didn't go very far.

Lundie, Doris Thayer, c. 1943, Kelso, Washington *(Thayer family photo)*

Lundie Thayer, c. 1941, *(Thayer family photo)*

CHAPTER 5

Employment

I've had a lot of jobs in my life. Some of them were good and some of them not so good. I'll tell you about my last, even though I still work all the time but nobody pays me. Anyway, Doris and I ran a meat business on Trout Creek Road outside Fort Washakie, Wyoming. When we moved there, there was nothin' but junk everywhere. By the time we left, there were two houses, a barn, a good orchard, and a meat plant that I built.

In the meat business, Doris took care of the books and wrapped the meat. I butchered the livestock and cut it up for her to wrap. We did custom meat processin' which meant the owners of the livestock or game told us how they wanted their meat to be cut and wrapped. We did that meat business for about thirteen years or so from 1976 to around 1989.

Karen moved on the place in 1991, but we quit runnin' the meat plant before then. I can't remember everything, but I do remember it was a good business. The Indian folks treated us right, and so did the white people. Both Doris and I were gettin' older and if age hadn't caught up with us, we'd still be runnin' that business. It just got to be too much—liftin' quarters of beef, skinnin' them, haulin' the bones and guts away. I enjoyed it especially since I could trust my wife to keep the books right and honest. We made out pretty good at Trout Creek Meat Processing Plant.

Before I built the slaughterhouse to butcher the animals, I ran a mobile slaughterhouse. Then I could either butcher at my home or at the customers' places. One time, a customer called me and wanted me to butcher his bull that had broke his leg. I told the customer I'd come with my mobile slaughterhouse. I used my old one-ton Chevy truck and put rails on the top and the sides. I had a hand-winch that I could pull anything with and it would raise the beef high enough to skin and dress him out. So I took my rig over to butcher the bull. When I got there, the bull was out on the side of the highway, way across the fence.

It was a muddy and wet time of year and looked like I should butcher the bull on the highway. The owner went across the fence to get around the bull, but the bull took out after him even with a broken leg. The owner ran as fast as he could before he fell down in the mud. Thank God I had my rifle loaded and laid it across the hood of my truck.

Well, this was one of the best shots I ever made. I hit that bull right between the eyes about 30 or 40 feet before it killed the owner, who was havin' trouble gettin' out of the mud. That customer, Ben O'Neal, thanked me a thousand times for savin' his life that day. Every time I'd see him, he'd thank me again. That was too close for comfort and pretty lucky with that .22 magnum rifle I still have to this day.

I took two chains and Ben brought a couple of chains so we could pull that bull out of the mud onto the highway and dress him out. When we got that job done, we saw Indian people comin' from both directions from Ethete and from the top of the hill to the north. Some of them would even drive around and then come back to see if the job was done. The Indian folks like tripe and entrails to eat, so we let 'em have 'em. Ben had to chase some of the people away since there was quite a crowd formin' and not enough guts for everyone. It's a good thing some people can eat what others can't; that way, nothin' gets wasted.

My son came and got the mobile slaughterhouse and still has it today. He's restorin' it 'cuz it's an antique built in 1964. We built the house in 1964 and the meat plant in 1974, so maybe they're antiques too. Doris and I sold the Trout Creek property to Karen in 1994, and she remodeled the meat plant into her home. She did a wonderful job and still invites me out to check on the place with her. I've got some good memories about the end of Trout Creek Road and I hope to have more.

I was a rancher for much of my life. In fact, the only time I didn't have anything to do with a ranch was when I was in the army. Before we moved to Trout Creek, Doris, the children and I lived on North Fork Road outside of Fort Washakie where we raised registered Polled Hereford cattle. In the summer, we'd run the cattle up on the range near Dickinson Park in the Wind River mountain range. It was close to 20 miles from our place to Dickinson Park. We trailed the cattle by saddle horse; that took about two or three days before we got there. We took our time 'cuz the cows might get weak and the calves were small. We ran them on the range from July 1 to October 1 each year for about four years.

The ranchin' business was good enough to keep our family fine. I sold plenty of registered bulls all over Wyoming and even shipped some back to Oregon. There's a lot of work to ranchin', but there's lots of satisfaction too. I sold the North Fork place to Gerry Spence, a lawyer that most people have heard about, and his wife, Imaging. The Spences have been my friends from that day to this. Our families always got along fine.

Ranch life can be really tragic too. My youngest son, Mark, was workin' for Gerry on another ranch near Dubois up on the East Fork. He and a buddy from Tennessee was movin' irrigation pipe one day when the pipe hit a power line and electrocuted them both right then and there. It was a very sad day for me and Doris and the Spences. Mark had plans to be an attorney, and Doris and I wanted to send him to school in California. But things changed and it's too sad to even talk about now.

Before we moved back to Wyoming, we lived on a ranch in Oregon. While on that ranch, I farmed and worked at a paper mill that was called the St. Helens Pulp and Paper Mill right there in St. Helens along the Columbia River pretty close to Doris' folks. I'd drive prittin' near five miles from our ranch to work at the paper mill for eight hours every day. After those hours and on the weekends, I'd manage our ranch, raisin' Polled Hereford cattle like I did later in Wyoming. In fact, I moved those Oregon cattle to Wyoming with me. 152 head of 'em were moved in two big trucks.

Workin' at the paper mill was my first job after I was discharged from the army. My first job at the paper mill was as a plugger. A plugger would put a wooden plug in each end of a roll of paper. Every roll had a plug so it wouldn't collapse. From a plugger, I went to first plugger and they did the same thing. From there, I went to bein' a fifth hand.

It's hard to explain unless you worked in a paper mill, but I'll try. The fifth hand took one end of a shaft that the paper was rolled, and the fourth hand would take the other end of the shaft that was made of steel. Then together, the fourth and fifth hands would take out the first shaft and put another shaft in its place. The reason shafts had to be replaced was 'cuz only a certain amount of paper could be rolled on one shaft. Fifth hands would move up to bein' a fourth hand in the line of seniority. From the fourth hand, I was moved up to winderman, who would be sure the paper was rollin' right on the shaft so the paper was right in line.

The size of the roll of paper varied dependin' on what the order called for. Sometimes, we'd have rolls as deep as 96 inches or 8 feet on one roll. We made butcher, wrappin', brown bag, fine line, and envelope paper on rolls. Each roll had a different weight of paper on it. Sometimes, the customer would order seven-pound paper, but we could make paper clear up to 250 pounds. The light paper of seven pounds was made into toilet tissue, napkins, writin' paper, and tissue like Kleenex. The middle weight paper most generally ran from 20 to 100 pounds and was used to make paper bags, newsprint, and construction paper or butcher paper. Of course, people could use any weight paper for whatever they were makin'. The heavy weight paper was made from 100 to 250 pounds and was called tagboard. It was used as covers on magazines or books, notebooks, milk cartons, and cardboard boxes 'cuz it was heavier and sturdier.

From winderman, the next position up was called back tender who was responsible to watch the weight, mullen, caliber, and finish of the paper. To make sure the weight was right, the back tender would use a scale to weigh a ream of paper that would determine the paper's assigned weight. The mullen was a machine that blew air up through the paper and when the pressure was great enough, the paper would tear and that spot was also called the mullen. The mullen was important 'cuz some companies ordered closed sheets and others ordered open sheets. You can't see through closed sheets, but with the open ones you can. Dependin' on the use of the paper, the customer would order either closed or opened. Envelope paper was made of closed or butcher paper, while the paper on sheetrock was open paper 'cuz it had to be glued to the sheetrock itself and the glue had to go through the paper to stick right. If any of these tests failed, the back tender needed to let the machine tender know immediately. The machine tender would make adjustments on the wet end. When I was a machine tender, I was over the whole outfit from the winder crew, the back tenders, the starch man, and the beader room where they ground the paper up until it came out like gravy and then added starch to help the finish of the paper. The finish of paper could be high-glaze, starch finish on all tag boards, or plain finish that had no starch. If paper was to be printed on, it was always better just to have plain finish. In the beader room, crew members took care of the color of paper and made sure it was right for the customer. I was a machine tender for close to four years after I worked my way to the top. Machine tenders made the most money 'cuz they had the most responsibility.

The only guy higher than machine tender was the tour boss who made sure all machines were workin' right. To get machinery repaired, the only person who could shut down operations was the tour boss. The tour boss also told all the new hires what the seniority process was so they always knew who their boss was and didn't get out of line.

The tour boss always said, "Don't come whinin' to me. Go to your own boss."

Now, what I'm tellin' you took me twenty-some years to learn, and that ain't all. Workin' at the paper mill was OK since I had a family to support. It was bread and butter on the table. But you know what? The whole time I was at the paper mill, I wanted to be back in Wyoming.

St. Helens Pulp and Paper sold out to Crown Zellerbach. One day, everything was goin' fine, but a man came into the machine room, didn't say a thing to anybody, and nobody knew who he was. He was a well-dressed elderly man who came up to one of the crew boys and asked, "How does that paper get its glaze?"

The crew boy said, "Beats the shit out of me. What the hell you askin' me for?"

The elderly man came to me and asked, "Can you tell me how the paper gets its glaze?"

I told him, "I'll try."

After I told him about the glaze process, the elderly man asked, "How long has that other boy been working here?"

I told him, "Oh, about three days."

He said, "That figures. He's got a ways to go. Thanks for the information," and he walked away.

The man's name was Zellerbach, the new owner of the paper mill. I don't think the crew boy would talk like that if he knew who he was talkin' to.

Later durin' my time at the paper mill, we found out that Crown Zellerbach had a monopoly on makin' paper all across the country. Crown Zellerbach had to sell the paper mill 'cuz there was a federal law against any business havin' a monopoly. So they sold to Boise-Cascade and I left the paper business for good.

But I still have a little notebook that I kept notes in to make sure I did the best job I could and not forget something important. There's notes on how to keep machines runnin' and how to use the equipment like raisin' the heads or settin' up the Jordon to help run the mullen. The whole business had its own vocabulary. I think all paper is made by computers now and not many of us men who knew how to do it are around anymore.

Even before I left the paper mill, we had a Machine #4 that had computers. But the computers didn't have to follow the seniority rules. So sure enough, one day, Machine #4 breaks down and there's no one to fix it. The union members, we called ourselves the Association of the Western Pulp and Paper Manufacturers, took the problem to the tour boss who told the superintendent who then said, "Hold those men over and have them put the wire on."

Well, the crew didn't know how to fix the wire and didn't want to. So the issue then went to the Grievance Committee of our union. The president of the Grievance Committee said, "Have the computer put the wire back on since it doesn't have any rules of seniority."

That's the only time I ever belonged to a union. They are a necessity even today for workers in these big corporations that get squeezed so the top dogs can make a fortune. I had many different jobs on many different ranches, but there weren't any unions for ranch hands. At that time, the whole country was in a Depression. A job was a job and everybody jumped for one if it came along. The goin' wage for a ranch hand was a dollar a day. And that day was full of hard work. If the boss said a workin' day was eight hours, they still could work us for 24 hours and pay us just for eight. Those bastards got by with it for a long time 'cuz we were in a Depression and had to take anything and everything. No unions were available to us.

Sometimes knowledge wasn't available to me either. When I was just a kid, I helped Carl Thompson take some of his cows to pasture. Carl had some land down on Dry Creek and he asked me if I'd take his cows down there. I told him I would, but I needed to know where I was headed and where the pasture was. Well, he looked at me and grinned. "There's a cabin down on Dry Creek. A lady lives there. The place is Rose's Hole. Take the cows down there and get directions from her about where the pasture is."

It was about twelve miles that I drove those cows before I came to Rosa's place. I knocked on the door and a lady came to the door. I asked her, "Is this Rose's Hole?"

She said, "You smart little SOB. You get the hell out of here, or I'll blow you out!"

I was shocked at the lady's reaction, but I kept on goin' to the next place. I asked those people, "Is this Rose's Hole?"

The man answered, "It's about another half-mile down this road. Just keep goin'."

I told him that I had asked the lady up the road the same question and she blew up at me, but I don't know what I said or did that was so wrong. The man asked what I had said to her. I told him all I asked was, "Is this Rose's Hole?"

The man busted up, asshole anyway. I didn't know what the big joke was until I was a lot older.

Rose was a fast lady like the other Rosa I told you about. Well, this Rose had the same job, but she worked for oil rig hands and drillers. They're the ones that hung the handle of Rose's Hole on her. I still don't think it's funny since all those adults were pickin' on me, just a boy whose Mama never learnt him anything like that or said anything like that.

Another job I had was runnin' a waterline in Cody on the Heart Mountain Canal Project. Our crew of about fourteen men ran the water liner through a big tunnel. The tunnel was about sixteen feet high and about fourteen feet wide and arched at the top. I had to drill four holes, each sixteen feet deep, straight into the rock. I worked with a crew of four men all together and each one of us had to drill four holes exactly sixteen feet long.

To get the job done, we used a water liner which was a machine that used high pressure water to turn the drill to get back sixteen feet. When our crew would get our sixteen holes drilled, the powder monkey would come along and load the holes with dynamite. That was a lot of dynamite, but we had a lot of rock to move too. The powder monkey had to be really smart and know just exactly how much dynamite to use in what hole. He also made sure that every hole was exactly sixteen feet. If it wasn't done right, you'd have to start over.

Along the track was a powder shack that was on four wheels and sat on the rails. Steel covered the whole thing with air holes comin' in and goin' out. When the dynamite was put in the holes, the powder monkey would jump in the powder shack next to us water liner operators. All of us would be in there and the powder monkey would push the plunger that blew all the holes. The dust and rocks from the explosions never reached us, but we made sure we were in the powder shack before anything blew. The main protection in the powder shack was from concussions caused by the pressure from the explosions and it had a constant source of good air.

The powder monkey had to time the explosions so that the bottom holes would blow first and the top holes would blow next. This task had to be timed really carefully so the tunnel would still have an arch to carry the water. After the powder monkey's job was done, the muckin' machine would come and clean up the muck—all the rocks or mud that was left after the explosion. We needed lots of water usin' the drills and the powder monkey made a lot of little rocks from the big rocks, which was called muck. The safety miner would come in to check that all sides and especially the top of the tunnel had no loose rocks that could fall and hurt the next crew.

The tunnel was built to carry water at the same time the Heart Mountain Canal was built. Both these projects were done to irrigate a bunch of sagebrush that was gonna be home to many newcomers. It was a development to encourage people to buy that land and farm it. The projects were probably done during WWII 'cuz they gave the returnin' veterans land around there under the GI Bill. The canal from this project carried water to the Japanese who were detained at Heart Mountain right after Pearl Harbor too.

The next tunnel I worked on was in Tucumcari, New Mexico, which was called the Conscious Irrigation Project. My brother Carl and I hitchhiked our way there 'cuz we still didn't have a car or a job, but we still had the Depression. We followed the same procedure as a water liner operator for the Heart Mountain Canal project. In fact, my boss on the Heart Mountain Canal project was the one who got us the jobs in New Mexico. For the Conscious Irrigation Project, they put us up in shacks by the job site. It was in that shack that I learnt the National Guard was gonna be inducted into federal service, so I headed back to Cody after workin' there only a little while.

That time, I didn't have to hitchhike even though Carl did 'cuz he had to get back to start school since he was only a teenager. While Carl was in Tucumcari, he grew fond of a little short-haired black dog he named Tucumcari. Carl hitchhiked back to Santa Fe with Tuppencary and finally got on a box car back to Cody 'cuz buses wouldn't allow his dog to go with him. I got to take a bus all the way home 'cuz the army paid for my ticket.

I got a job rip-rappin' on the Cody Canal. Just like roadways have to have slopes to keep moisture from washin' the bank out, canals have to have slopes too. So I was layin' rocks on the side of the Cody Canal for probably two months. It was a good job, hard work, but they paid me $1.25 a day which was fine by me. Any job was good.

I hated the next job I had, but I had to take it. A guy named Whitey asked me if I wanted a job. Whitey said, "I have a contract haulin' cement for the Heart Mountain Tunnel."

I said, "Sure."

He said, "I'll give you $1.25 a day."

"Fine," says I.

Whitey's contract was with a construction company to use his flatbed truck and a trailer to haul loads of cement sacks. The cement came into Cody on the railroad and we'd haul the sacks from the boxcars on Whitey's rig to the tunnel where it would be stockpiled until crews could line the whole tunnel, top to bottom, with cement. There was 60,000 pounds to the boxcar load. Believe it or not, Whitey and I would unload one boxcar, just the two of us, in ten hours. It would take us two trips with the truck and flatbed. We figured each of us had moved fifteen tons.

Now, I was a young, strapping' man less than 21 years old and full of muscles except no brains. I'll tell you the truth—there was a time unloadin' that cement that I could carry by myself two bags, each one weighing 80 pounds. That's true. And this was the only damn job I ever had that I couldn't get myself clean. That cement always stuck to my skin, all over my face and arms. It was really filthy and I'd had some pretty dirty jobs before.

My next job was from home in Cody, night-lambin', for Mr. Heald. Well, I was watchin' to be sure that all the ewes and their new lambs were paired up and put in a jug together. Not a jug of water, but a jug that was a small fenced pen, about 4 x 6 feet.

One night just before dark, it started to snow real hard. Those old ewes kept poopin' little lambs out one right after another. I got all the jugs filled and there was still more baby lambs comin', so I had to move the sheep from the jugs into a holdin' pen. And still, lambs kept comin'. The whole sheep shed was filled up. Plus lots of the drop herd, ewes who still hadn't dropped their babies, were still out in the corral.

There wasn't any room left in the shed for mamas or babies, but the snow kept comin'. It was already about two to three feet deep and baby lambs don't do good in snow that deep. They're dead. So I drove the drop herd up under the eaves of the sheep shed to give them some protection and a place to have their babies where they might survive. Well, wouldn't you know it? That snow came off the sheep shed's steel roof in one big sheet and landed right on that whole drop herd.

I went to the house and told Mr. Heald what happened. Mr. Heald woke up all the other hands and told them to get out there and save those sheep. We worked hard and fast to keep those sheep from suffocating under all that snow. And our work paid off, we lost only a couple of ewes. I worked my heart out tryin' to keep up with all those babies, but the other hands were pissed at me for puttin' the sheep under the eaves in the first place. Mr. Heald thought I did right to try to save those lambs.

Another job I got was herdin' 30 head of cows up to the head of Wood River above Meeteetse. Sam Riley offered the job to me and I took it in a heartbeat. That job took about three days and I came home as a millionaire. I had $3, $1 a day and I was filthy rich.

Once, I had a job haulin' manure which you could think was a filthy job, but it wasn't. We got $5 a pick-up load in my buddy's Model A pick-up. Chuck Evans and I had a good business especially for the spring of the year. We used to get this manure on bed grounds, where the sheep bedded down all winter, and most generally, the sheep men would just give it to us. Why? Because by taking away the manure, the sheep were cleaner and less prone to disease. We'd deliver the manure to many people in Cody.

If all the manure was stood up against each other—horse, cow, goat, chicken, anything—the best is sheep manure 'cuz it was in small pellets and it's easy to handle and spread. It also broke down easy in the spring with the first rain. Some of the Cody people who took our sheep shit ended up being kind of famous. We sold to Jakey Schobe, who ran the Cody Trading Company; Milward Simpson, who was father to a U.S. Senator; Ernest Goppert, who was an attorney like Simpson; Mr. Molesworth, a furniture tycoon; Charlie Taggart, who owned a construction company; and several others.

Our most regular customer was Mrs. Oskins who ran a greenhouse between Cody and the CBQ (Chicago, Burlington, and Quince) Railroad Depot. Mrs. Oskins raised flowers and a few vegetable plants to sell locally. Boy, she knew how to grow things usin' sheep manure, which was her only fertilizer. Any time we got an extra load of sheep manure, she'd buy it.

I'm glad I had all these different jobs. Even though they didn't pay much, I learnt a lot of different things that helped me throughout my life. Hard work was something I tried to teach my kids. Honesty comes from hard work too. Even though honesty doesn't have a dollar sign, it's worth a million bucks.

CHAPTER 6

Gardening

Of course, everyone gardens in different ways, but no one can deny you have to work at it. So I'll give you a couple of tips about soil preparation first since that's where all good gardens begin. You can either plow, spade, or rototill your garden plot. The idea is to break up the soil and prepare the dirt to take the seeds. Be sure to cultivate the whole garden space at least eight inches deep. By turning the soil over, you can mix up any sand or clay. My main thing to make a good soil is to put at least three inches of manure on top of the garden before you spade or plow.

Like I told you before, sheep manure is good, but any manure will do. Make sure the manure is aged for at least two years before you spread it. Don't put it on your garden hot or fresh 'cuz it will burn the seeds and nothin' will grow except weeds.

You want to be sure to turn the soil over before winter sets in too. That kills any weed seeds that you missed and it will hold any compost or leftover garden that makes the soil rich for the next spring. Be sure to turn the soil twice, once in the spring before plantin' and once after you harvest.

Some people don't like rocks in their gardens. I think some rocks if they're small enough can actually help a garden to hold its moisture. Sand works the same way except it helps the water get to the roots.

Let's go on to plantin'. Take your time before you plant and make sure the soil is prepared right. You need to be sure you have the right amount of moisture in the ground that will germinate the seeds. Too much water will drown the seeds and not enough will stop 'em from germinatin'. You can pre-sprout some seeds. Some plants just won't pre-sprout like watermelon, cantaloupe, cucumbers, and all the melon family. Any other seed will usually pre-sprout. Make sure you don't just take the sprout and plant it. You need to test the seed and the sprout to see if the plant will actually germinate. Why go to all the work to plant a garden if the seeds are bad? I'll tell you more about seeds later.

Now, I want to tell you about waterin'. Be sure to keep the soil damp but not wet. Being too wet will drown the seed and the sprout which could make 'em rot. If the seed gets too dry, I found out that if you dampened 'em down a little, they'll come back and be as good as they were in the first place. Be careful not to drown the seeds 'cuz then they'll never come back. If they do come back, the fruit won't grow right 'cuz they're sick. That goes for any plant too. Being too wet has killed more plants than any weed or wind ever did.

I'm against chemicals and in favor of insects to pollinate plants. Manure does the fertilizin' and lady bugs, ants, or any bug that comes along can be helpful to you in the garden. This is true 'cuz some other bug will be its enemy if it's not gonna help the garden. These bug-killer chemicals will take care of endin' life for all of us in the long run. I've found out that by usin' tobacco juice, just a mix of tobacco and water, will take care of all the weed killin' you'll ever need in a garden. Don't mix it too strong; just mix it lightly with water and you'll see what I mean. It takes care of aphids and other bad bugs that can't hatch out in tobacco juice. It won't kill ants, lady bugs or good bugs. Be careful if you use tobacco juice on weeds 'cuz you may mix it too strong and then it will harm the good plants too. I'm a strong believer in just lettin' Mother Nature do some of the work in the garden.

We can all know what's in the food from our gardens. Food in the stores may come from China, Mexico, or anywhere in the world and those countries may use chemicals we may not even know about. Look at how much cancer and illness we have anymore; it's just the way it is now. I don't remember any cancer or illnesses like we have today when I was a kid. Maybe it's in the food we eat.

Mama never gave us vaccines or shots and we all survived. Maybe these shots are what's causin' cancer. Who knows? I'm not a scientist or a doctor, but I do know how to think and I sure as hell don't trust chemicals. Anything to make a dollar could be what's hurting us. These companies will make anything to sell you if it will make them a dollar.

To prove it, listen up. I remember when the bald eagle was an endangered species. The government passed a law to quit using DDT, a strong chemical that used to kill bugs, that they sprayed from airplanes, on gardens, huge growing plots and it got in the water too. Well, it was about 20-25 years after they banned DDT that the bald eagle started to come back. Thank God 'cuz I like those birds. That's just one example, but it proves that chemicals are no good.

When it comes down to gardens and chemicals, I'm an environmentalist. Aren't we all environmentalists if we care about what's livin' around us?

Anyway, back to plantin'. Be sure to space the seeds in a proper row. I plant my rows from three to four feet apart. Even then, I have to thin the rows sometimes. This much space between 'em gives me a chance to cultivate or turn the soil while the plants are still young. It gives the plants more room to grow too and you're not wastin' seeds. I always keep plants, even if I have to thin 'em, about three and a half to four and a half inches apart. This is really important to keep the color in plants 'cuz if seeds grow too thick, they take the nutrients out of the soil and rob the goodness from another row of plants.

A honey bee likes color and humans like food, so we need to have bees to have our food 'cuz they pollinate the plants for us. I was havin' trouble one year in my garden on Boulder Flats 'cuz there weren't any honeybees. I guess that's happenin' in a lot of places. Too bad 'cuz we really need 'em if we want to eat.

Anyway, I took some old plastic artificial flowers from my family's graves in Cody and just put 'em on the fence around my garden. Sure enough, the bees came back and have been here since which always helps you get a lot of food from a garden. They're great pollinizers. We need bees and butterflies that help spread pollen.

When you're ready to harvest, do it when the plants are ripe— usually in the fall. I say the plants above ground need to be harvested before the first frost and the plants below ground you can harvest after the first frost. That's about all there is to harvestin'.

I'm talkin' about just plain gardenin' without babyin' it. Lots of people baby their gardens by coverin' with sheets or other stuff, which anyone can do, but sometimes it won't help anyway 'cuz the plants will always ripen when they're good and ready.

Something I do at harvest time is to keep my own seed. I find out that my seed, those that I keep, will grow better the next year 'cuz the seed is used to the soil. In order to get my own seed, I pick the seed from the plant and air-dry 'em. That's to say, take only the seeds, not the stems or leaves or roots, just the seeds of any above-ground plant. To air dry 'em right, spread 'em out in an even layer. Don't stack 'em and let nature do the work. I don't ever stick seeds in the oven, although I guess other gardeners have. After the seeds are good and dry and separated, I put 'em in a glass jar or a plastic bag to keep for next spring. In the spring, before the seeds go into the ground, I test germinate 'em to be sure they'll make in the garden.

Another important thing is to always plant your seeds in the same soil they came from. My seeds are mostly from Wyoming and my own garden. That's probably why the garden produces so well for me. My potatoes are grown in the same spot until I rotate 'em, which is about every other year. The seeds are still from the same garden soil even though they're not from exactly the same spot in the garden every year. Since there are different nutrients in different areas of the garden, you're best to rotate plantin' different things in different areas so they all can get the nutrients.

Now, root crops are a different story. Take potatoes for an example. They're a root crop. To produce your own potatoes, take the potato eyes, which are the seeds that don't need to be dried. Carrots are a root crop too, but their seeds are above ground and they will reseed themselves if given a chance. So will lettuce, rutabaga, beets, and spinach. Potatoes are funny since they're the only plant I know of that goes to seed on the potato itself–on its own eyes.

I have a story about the potato. I heard this woman tell her daughter to get back in the house when she came out to the garden without her pants. The mama said, "Girl, don't you know those potatoes have eyes?" That's just a little joke. Don't think I'm crazy.

OK, back to gardenin'. Enough jokin' around.

When you're ready to put your garden food away for the winter like onions, potatoes, carrots, parsnips, and anything that grows below ground, put 'em in separate bins. Make sure they stay nice and cool with plenty of air circulation. Don't wash the dirt off any of 'em 'cuz it protects 'em through the long winter. Just make sure they're dry. If you don't, the vegetables will sprout, go soft and rot so you can't eat 'em. I've only lost a few vegetables over the winter and it was 'cuz I had bought bad seeds in the first place.

Before you put vegetables up for the winter, be sure to cut off the tops down to about an inch, about the width of your thumb from the vegetable itself. They have to be cool with lots of air all winter. And be sure you sort them every once in a while durin' the winter. Throw out any that are rotten or turnin' soft 'cuz those soft ones will ruin the others too.

Every time Mama told us to go to the cellar to get vegetables, she'd say, "Be sure to use the rule of thumb," which meant to go through the bin or sack and get rid of the bad ones. We knew this was important so we'd have food for the rest of the winter.

It's important to know how to prune a tree too. Keep all the dead branches cut off every tree. Make sure you cut off all the branches that are crossin' each other too. That way, the sunlight can get to the entire tree. Trim the lower branches off over a period of years, which helps the tree grow taller and thicker. I never cut the lower branches above six feet, which gives the trunk room to grow bigger and the appearance is better too.

On fruit trees, never cut off the fruit spurs, which is where the fruit grows out of the branch. Prunin' is best in the cooler months. Never prune from February to September. Now, if a fruit tree limb gets broke, there's three things you can do. Just cut it off completely and put paint or tree wax on the wound. To wrap a tree limb, take a piece of clean cloth and wrap the branch back up on the tree. This may take a couple of rags, but just keep it wrapped until it heals and is part of the tree again. The tree wax, the paint, and wrappin' help seal the tree's sap in the tree instead of all the tree's life bleedin' out. Sometimes a tree can actually bleed to death. If the wound doesn't heal, it will just drip and drip and drip until there's no more sap. Just like a cut on your finger, you want to seal the blood in with a band aid. Do this on any tree if the limb is not already dead. If it's dead already, just cut it off.

Now, one of the most important tips about any plant is the water. If you can possibly give your house plants, gardens and pastures water that is lukewarm, you'll have better results. One of the most shockin' things to any plant is cold water. That shocks especially new plants more than anything else. To prove my point, just think about this. When you take a bath, you'd rather be in warm water. Cold water shocks you silly too, just like plants. That's how I like to think about plants, especially house plants. They're just like people. It's the truth that if you're workin' real hard on a hot day, a fresh cool rain shower feels good. But if you're cold to start with, nothin' is more shockin' than more cold water on top of that.

CHAPTER 7

Places

I've been so lucky to see some of the Earth's most beautiful places and some of the ugliest too. Old stories from England will start us off. I learned a scary story that happened in England from readin' an old newspaper. There were men who peddled silk and other fabrics in the old days there. They'd walk the streets or use a wagon to sell their wares. Over time, several of those silk merchants came up missin'. Well, this is what I read in an old newspaper clippin' that was handed down to my family from my great-grandma, Grannie Specks.

A lady and her son lived together where the silk merchants used to visit while sellin' their silk. Come to find out, once in the house, the son would hit the merchants in the head and the mother would take all the silk and sell it. They killed at least ten people, since Grandma said they found that many skeletons.

But the scariest part of this story is the mother and her son would take the human flesh, pickle and can it, then sell it to the higher-ups at a premium price. They also made pickled pork 'cuz they raised hogs. I wonder if the higher-ups knew the difference between human and pork since all the meat was sold as pork.

As punishment, the clippin' said the couple were staked to the ground and starved. Anyone who tried to feed them got staked to the ground too.

Another England story was about hangin' people. I read an article that said one hangman saved a lot of lives. He'd take a wedge, put it under the hangin' platform, so when the rope was pulled, the platform would not release. Back then, they thought if the trap door didn't go down, the person was innocent. Finally, the officials found out what he was doin' and they hung him.

I was born in an interestin' place—a ghost town, really. Old Arland was a famous wild west town for several years. But it went too wild and everyone moved out except Pete Peron. My folks took a job in Old Arland to take care of Pete when I was born and became Pete's Little Man. Pete, my folks, and my family was the only people in Old Arland when I showed up in 1915.

A sign along the road between Meeteetse and Cody tells folks about Old Arland and its wild history. The sign says Old Arland was only a town for about thirteen years and was one of the toughest towns in western history with a post office, a two-story hotel, a tradin' company and corrals. Black Jack Miller, John Bliss, Al Durant, and Butch Cassidy were residents at different times. Bill Holligan, Ed Neigh, Sagebrush Nancy, and Nellie Dreary, the woman known as the Woman in Blue, died there entangled in a web of romance, intrigue and murder. By 1896, the nearby town of Meeteetse had sprung up which put an end to Old Arland by 1897.

Around Meeteetse, there's another interestin' place. It's a sad place that Mama told me about. When the Spanish flu of 1917 or so hit, lots of ranchin' folks caught it and died. There's a draw east of Meeteetse where they're buried. Mama said the wagons haulin' the dead came right by her place. I don't remember it at all, but the hill is still there with lots of bones in it, I imagine. The schools were quarantined and people were isolated in their own homes for months at a time.

I've told you about my great-grandmother settlin' Fenton, Wyoming, which was the town about fifteen miles east of Meeteetse along the road to Burlington. The road follows the Greybull River to the town my great-grandmother founded. You can also take the road from Greybull, headin' west to Fenton. Some maps have Fenton Pass marked on 'em, which is where my great-grandmother got lost comin' from Salt Lake. She kept goin' until she got to the Greybull River, which is why she started the town of Fenton there 'cuz it had plenty of water.

The Oregon Basin is an interestin' place along the road to Cody from Meeteetse. The oldest oil rig in Wyoming is at Oregon Basin sittin' right along the road and is still in operation today. There's a lot to see out there in all that sagebrush and a lot of history to learn about that area too. You may not believe me, but I've found elk horns, mountain sheep horns, deer horns, and even some kind of bear skeleton out in that country. There's been a lot of wildlife through there in olden times and now it's great cattle country with lots of oil rigs too.

Dead Indian Mountain was the place I packed supplies to for two sheep camps and a cow camp that George Heald owned. That mountain got its name as I was told 'cuz it was the last battle the cavalry had with the Crow Indians. That's about all I know about that place.

Another place was called Francs Peak, which I thought was named for my grandfather, Frank Lundie. Now days, the modern maps have that place named Franc's Peak which was named for Otto Franc, a big landowner in those parts. I'm not sure on it, but the old timers connected Frank's Peak to my grandfather with no word said about any Otto Franc.

I don't know how Greybull got its name. Grannie Specks heard about the Greybull River while she was in Salt Lake City, Utah. But I don't know how the name Greybull came about. There's the Greybull Meadows too which is where Shanks Maddox and I doctored that Hereford bull with a big wound that I previously mentioned. The Greybull River starts at the head of Sunshine Reservoir. Meeteetse Creek runs into the Greybull River, but modern maps have very different names than what I knew growin' up there and from what the old-timers always said.

Some maps have the names I know like Wiley, which is between Meeteetse and Cody not too far from the Two Dot Ranch and where my family homesteaded between Wiley and the Two Dot. We used to live in a house at Wiley, but that house was moved to Cody and now sits on Main Street and is called the Green Gables.

Thayer Junction was named for part of my family who settled in southern Wyoming near Rock Springs. My grandfather's brother started a tradin' post there where he traded sound livestock to pioneers who were migratin' to California or Oregon. He'd fatten up the poor livestock out near Horse Thief Canyon and trade 'em again. When the railroad came through, my family's business went under, but the place is still identified as Thayer Junction even on some modern maps.

Like a lot of families, some of the Thayers migrated too. Part of the Thayer Junction family made it to Oregon and one of 'em became governor of Oregon, but I don't know his name for sure. I do know that some of 'em settled near Mount St. Helens where one of my distant relatives was killed in 1980 when Mount St. Helens blew its top. I was talkin' to Mr. McCoy in 1942 and he knew about the Thayer Junction Thayers that I ended up meeting in 1947.

Another story I want to tell you about is a place called Crandell Creek with no post office or anything. How it got its name was 'cuz an old prospector hunted for gold in that creek and he did very well. Crandell Creek was named for him. It was a wild place back in the old days. All of Wyoming was wild then.

I remember hearin' the story about Crandell Creek and later seein' a book about Crandell Creek. Well, the cavalry was lookin' for Mr. Crandell 'cuz no one had seen him for a while. Sure enough, they found him—at least, his head. Someone had cut off his head and put it on a rock with a brand new cupful of water in front of the head. The cavalry knew immediately that this was an old Indian trick and started huntin' for the people who killed Mr. Crandell. Well, they found several Indians and hung them right on the spot 'cuz they admitted their crime.

Most cavalry units were accompanied by friendly Indians who could speak the English language and the Indian dialect too. So these Indian guides could interpret for the cavalry and helped 'em find the guilty Indians. To this day, Mr. Crandell's source of gold has never been discovered. I even looked for it several times when I was out ridin' through that area.

Now, let me tell you about Butter Bowl Basin. By the way, it's the headwaters of Crandell Creek and is a real beautiful area. It's out of this world with all the wildflowers; and, all summer long, the peaks are covered with snow. I used to love watchin' the new baby lambs romp and jump and play. Pretty soon, the wild sheep's little lambs would join 'em in their rompin' while the adult sheep licked the salt that I had packed in for the sheepherders and cowboys. I would sit and watch 'em for hours with my black dog, Tip.

One day, while I was watchin' the lambs, I decided to try to snare a rock chuck. Sure enough, he stuck his head out, and I snared him with the bacon string they used to wrap hams with. Well, he turned out to be a great pet, old Chucky. I spoiled him with Carnation milk from a can. When I'd ride back into my camp after leavin' him there on his own, he'd greet me with a bark and keep barkin' until I got him back into the cabin where he lived with me and I could pour him some milk.

Chucky came to a bad end, though, 'cuz Tip had made friends with a red fox. Boy, they sure named the fox right 'cuz they can outfox any of us. Anyway, Chucky and the fox were Tip's friends, and both of 'em would eat the food I put out for Tip. I'd watch all day and the only time I'd see that fox was when it was Tip's dinnertime. Sure enough, that fox was there every day. One day, either the fox or Tip killed Chucky and ate him. All I found was one of his little hind legs.

Butter Bowl Basin was always so beautiful. I really enjoyed myself there. You talk about goin' to heaven—well, I've been there. All by myself in that wonderful open air and big mountains sure was heaven to me. Ended up bein' heaven for my pet Chucky too. When I packed for Heald for three years, I always looked forward to goin' to Butter Bowl. I heard that the basin got its name 'cuz it was created by a volcano and it looked just like a great big bowl.

Pat O'Hara Mountain, outside of Cody, is where my brother Sid worked for Mr. Demoriak as the boss over sheep and cattle herds. I don't know who Pat O'Hara was or why a mountain was named for him, but I do know some things that happened in that area.

Sid hired a man named Earl Duran to herd sheep. Sid and I were deliverin' groceries and sheep salt to him once when he was herdin' sheep on Pat O'Hara Mountain. Mr. Duran told Sid, "I hope one of you guys can herd sheep 'cuz I'm takin' off right now to walk through Yellowstone Park over to Idaho and make a big circle back to Powell. You can send me my pay when I get back."

That was it. So Sid just left me there alone to herd those 2,400 head of sheep which was my first time as a sheepherder while he went to find Mr. Duran's replacement. All my brothers taught me to do things the best I could even if I was still a kid. They made me grow up and use my wits.

Well, Pat O'Hara Mountain is full of mysteries. One of the mysteries is about potatoes. Believe it or not, my brother Sid and his buddy, Ted Feeley, grew an acre of the biggest, reddest potatoes I'd ever seen. And they grew 'em in that high country. I still can't figure out how, but I sure ate a lot of 'em.

Now, that's a mystery, but another Pat O'Hara potato mystery happened when the Feeley family stored some of those red potatoes in a root cellar behind the Cody Trading Company. Ted, his wife, and his two brothers went down to the cellar to sort the potatoes like you have to do with all vegetables so they don't rot. As they went in the cellar, Ted struck a match to light a lantern. Boom, the whole place blew up. The explosion took the whole dirt roof off that cellar. A person outside the cellar could look straight down on the potatoes that weren't hurt or burned at all. One or two of them scattered around, but that's all that happened to those potatoes.

The ground had frozen and the natural gas line that came into one of the Main Street stores there in Cody leaked into that potato cellar. When a match was lit, there she went. Of course, we had no electricity in those days. All we had was kerosene lanterns and carbide lights that we used at home.

What's so mysterious is that two Feeleys boys' hair got scorched, but they were really OK. Two others weren't so lucky. They ended up with brain damage and were never the same after that cellar blew up. Some of them lost every hair on their heads, but not Ted. Everyone said that Ted was protected 'cuz he had his cowboy hat on. He never did find that hat after the blast though. Most of us Thayer kids went to the cellar and sacked the potatoes up so they wouldn't freeze overnight. I, myself, saw that cellar without a roof when I helped to salvage the good potatoes, but I never saw Ted's hat.

The community really came together to help the Feeleys by buyin' every one of those potatoes. Sid gave his share to sell too, just to help the family. Back in those days, the people were really good to one another. Of course, there were some that were really, really bad too. We learnt to stay away from 'em.

Everyone back then had a college education even if we didn't go to high school. The name of the college we graduated from during the Depression was Herbert Hoover University. We all learned poverty, starvation and unemployment by the millions. Herbert Hoover was a real SOB to lots of people. But, sometimes I think if he hadn't taught us those hard lessons and how we shared and worked to help each other, we would have ended up a lot weaker. Our Herbert Hoover University education made us strong and our community stronger.

Oh yeah, I was tellin' you about Mr. Duran and I want to finish his story. Here's what took place. Mr. Duran killed an elk out of season. The game warden arrested him and took him to Cody to answer to the charges. Well, the justice of the peace sentenced Mr. Duran to jail, but Mr. Duran had lived his whole life independently as a real loner.

Duran had shot many a deer, elk, antelope—you name it—in the past before the law was to have licenses for each kill. Mr. Duran didn't even know you had to have a license, but that made no difference to the justice of the peace and Duran's jail sentence.

While Mr. Duran was in jail, the deputy sheriff brought him a meal. Mr. Duran knocked the deputy in the head with a milk bottle and made him open the cell. And Mr. Duran made the deputy drive him to Powell. When the deputy left Mr. Duran at his home, the deputy notified the Powell Sheriff, Mr. Baker, who in turn notified his deputy, Mr. Lindenberry, about Mr. Duran's arrival in Powell. Baker and Lindenberry went to pick Duran up by sneakin' down a dry canal before they hollered, "Duran, surrender!"

When they stuck their head above the canal bank, Duran shot 'em both with a 30 x 30 rifle, killin' 'em both. Duran then took off for the mountains that he knew so well.

By that time, the Park County Sheriff had been alerted to the Duran case and gathered up a posse. The posse cornered Duran in a small canyon in the vicinity of the Bear Tooth Mountains. Mr. Argento and Mr. Lewis were members of the posse and told Duran to surrender. Duran warned the posse to leave; they refused and both men were killed instantly by Duran. Duran took the men's shoelaces and tied the two corpses together before he took off headin' for the highway between Powell and the Montana state line.

Duran caught a ride with the same man that wouldn't pick up Carl and me as kids when we were tryin' to walk home after the snake rattle got us bucked off. That same Hanson man would pick up a murderer, but he wouldn't pick up two young barefooted boys.

Anyway, back to the Mr. Duran story. By this time, the whole community was alerted and the murders had even made national radio news. Everyone was to be on the lookout for Duran. And here, he sat in the back seat of Hanson's car.

Finally, Mr. Duran asked Hanson, "What would you do if you saw Duran?"

Hanson answered, "I'd shoot him if I had a gun."

Duran said, "Well, you better look in your back seat then."

Hanson almost fainted 'cuz a known murderer was right behind him.

Mr. Duran said, "You just keep drivin' to Powell and stop in front of the bank there."

When Hanson's vehicle pulled up in front of the bank, Mr. Duran said, "You go ahead and peddle your cookies 'cuz I'm goin' in here."

Mr. Duran took his 30 x 30 rifle, walked in the bank, and started shootin' the hell out of the building but not the people. People said he went "bear sick," which is to say he lost his mind in jail 'cuz he was in an enclosed area and wasn't used to that kind of space.

There was one person from my class at school that tried to stop Mr. Duran. We always thought of him as a timid person. His name was Johnny Garthrup. Duran killed him too and then walked out of the bank and started down the street. Some kid on the roof of a nearby store shot and killed Mr. Duran puttin' an end to his five-man killin' spree.

In those days, people were in favor of hunters' rights and against licensin' and all the new laws that were comin' into effect. So to many people, Mr. Duran was kind of a hero. He was to our family 'cuz we needed to hunt when we needed to eat, whether it was a legal season or not. Mr. Duran had a lot of support by the local people. In fact, I heard from two men that sat right down next to Mr. Duran after he killed Argento and Lewis to share a breakfast with him. No one turned Duran in then 'cuz so many people were used to the old ways and hated the new laws.

The kid who finally killed Duran had to leave Powell 'cuz so many people were in favor of Duran that they feared the kid and his family would be killed as revenge for killin' Duran. I also heard that Mr. Duran had told the sheriffs and deputies that when they killed him, he wanted them to cut off his head and mount it at the Park County Courthouse with the following statement underneath. "For law, order, and peace. Earl Duran."

The freight line that my dad took for all those years had some interestin' places too. The first campsite was the bottom of Meeteetse Creek Rim; the next was at Chipmunk Gap where there is a sign today tellin' about the old freight stop that was run on that very spot. The next campsite was at Dry Creek which is off the current highway and you can't really see it but it ran right through the middle of the old Thayer homestead. The fourth campsite was right in Korbit where my dad would unload the freight. Yep, it took three nights and four days of travel by horse team to get from Meeteetse to Cody.

Then the freight was loaded on a ferry to cross the Stinkin' Water (Shoshone) River where a Montana freight business would take over and get the load on to Billings. Freight teams were like early railroads and the work was hard. After the railroad came in, a lot more things moved a lot faster and a lot easier.

Wind River Mountains, Trout Creek Canyon, 2018 *(Karen King Photo)*

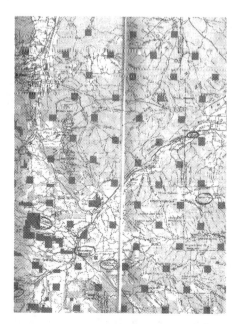

Wyoming map showing Fenton, Fenton Pass, Long Hollow,
Wiley, Meeteetse, and Cody *(Gazetter Map, 1999)*

Business at North Fork

The red-tailed hawk laid spread-eagle in the dust
At the front door steps of Lundy Thayer's house.
Its blood had dried, its eyes as big and red as rusty dimes,
And in a first look and quick turning away
What was the color of dried blood
And the color of feathers was hard to say.

The red-tailed hawk had company.
Three feet to the south laid the smiling, severed head
Of last year's Herford calf, lately of the freezer,
Also red-brown, staring back at Lundy Thayer
With big, flat eyes, turning green as half dollars.

"Ya see my old tom cat in the trees over there?"
Asked Lundy Thayer.
"Where?"
"That black thing hanging there is my old tom.
That hawk grabbed him by his hair,
And kilt him dead as hell with one big swoop.
But he couldn't make it over the trees,
So he just dropped him. And there he hangs.
Good place fer a cat ta die," Lundy surmised.
Then laughed.

The old tom looked like a gentle, swaying Jolly Roger
Or maybe a mourner's armband ripped from some descending ghost,
Or, say, a pair of witch's worsted panties.
But it was the old tom all right.
Up close his eyes were as large and flat as chocolate-red quarters.
He was looped over a willow branch
About fifteen feet off the ground, tail and head together
Like a swan diver frozen with a belly cramp.

Well, it just seemed right to me.
I argued that it came out fair.
Lundy was the winner.

He lost his help to catch the mouse
But he was a damn good shot
And got the red-tail from the front steps
Of his house with his twelve gauge
And had calf's liver for supper.

Gerry Spence
May 20, 1971

Poem "Business on North Fork" by Gerry Spence, 1971

The Teton Range, 2016 *(Karen King photo)*

The Shoshone River, 2014 *(Karen King photo)*

CHAPTER 8

Cures

Well, I know some animal cures and cures for humans too. Let's start with animal cures. I told you about the salt and iodine water Shanks Maddox and I used on that old bull and it worked great. It will also work great on any animal since it stops infection. Wire cut, laceration, or any open wound on any animal can be protected by usin' just good old water, salt, and iodine. Problem is, you can't buy iodine anymore which is a real shame. Seems they want you to only go to vets and pay through the nose for something you could fix yourself.

Another good cure was pine tar that worked good at preventin' infections in animals. You can't find the ingredients anymore either. But, a long time ago, we used to get tar that was real black and made out of real pine. The tar you get these days is made from crude oil like you use to roof a house—not pine tar. This current tar won't work. My preference is salt, iodine, and water 'cuz if the wound is infected with maggots, it will drive all the maggots out and kill all the eggs too. Be sure to keep the iodine water away from any animal's eyes. It would do more damage there than good.

You see, they've taken care of that now too with penicillin and all these antibiotics. These old cures was all we had before the vets and drugs showed up. We had cures for poisoned animals too.

If any animal got poisoned, we always used dry mustard and water. Now, these old cures with dry mustard and water would make the animal throw up and the mixture would have a tendency to neutralize the poison. It's especially good to use on dogs or cats and small animals. Just be sure to get it down 'em. We used to take any damned thing to get it down 'em. The sooner you get it in 'em, the stronger your chance of savin' the animal.

Mama used to use an empty quart whiskey bottle and it would go down the dog's throat easier since the bottle had a longer neck on it. By God, you better force it down 'em fast. They don't like it, but it usually saves their lives. Mama used to make a kinda liquid gravy that she just poured down their throats. The more mustard, the stronger the liquid.

A medium-sized dog should have at least a cupful, but more won't hurt them. The animal will puke right away and if they seem to feel better, just keep watch on 'em. If they don't feel better, give 'em another dose right away. The mustard won't hurt 'em, but if the poison or strychnine gets through the animal's system, he'll likely die. Get it in 'em as soon as you can.

Now, I had a cat named Sweety Plum who got to feelin' poorly. She was old, but I wanted her around as long as possible. So I mixed any ole type of vinegar with milk 'cuz it would sour her stomach immediately and she would puke up whatever was botherin' her. I used an old syringe to get it down her throat; she didn't mind it. She got to feelin' better within three or four hours after she vomited.

This same cat was gettin' really old, so I took some raw hamburger and mixed it with some milk, made gravy out of it and fed it to her with a teaspoon. Sure enough, she got stronger for a while. I did take her to the vet who said she had probably eaten some spoiled mice that may have been poisoned by mice bait. I was tryin' everything I knew to save that wonderful cat, but she died curled up on my bed. I still miss her.

I'll tell you about a blood stopper that can be used on animals or humans. Take a cup of flour, put it on the stove and keep stirrin' it until it turns brown. Then after it's brown, let it cool off and pour some iodine in it until you have a paste. If your horse or human has a wound that is bleeding really bad, put it directly in the wound. Don't be afraid to use a lot and press it in a little. Put a bandage or rag around it kind of tight and leave it for as long as it keeps bleedin'.

Mama used to call this an instant scab that would protect the wound and stop the bleedin'. When you take the bandage off, you'll see a nice black scab from the iodine, which also protects the wound from infection. Now, the reason you brown the flour is to sterilize it and not cause more infections.

Good luck findin' iodine. Some people say to use salt since it's iodized and about the only way to get your hands on iodine now days. If you make about half a cup of salty solution by dissolvin' three or four tablespoons of table salt in hot water, then pour that into the wound it could help fight infection. Salt is good on sore teeth and gums in animals and humans too.

We never had aspirin when I was a kid. All we had was quinine which came from the South Pacific islands somewhere. During WWII, all the medicines in all the hospitals were confiscated for military use. Quinine had been used for malaria to save thousands of men in tropical places. We used it to relieve pain. Mama wouldn't ever use quinine 'cuz she called it a dangerous drug 'cuz it was used durin' surgeries, so she knew it was really strong. When the Japs stopped the supply lines that quinine had to travel, we couldn't get it anymore. That's when the military started usin' "laughing gas."

You know, we have lots of smart people in this country. They invented penicillin and other medicines to help during WWII. Too bad we don't use our smarts anymore. We could stop any illness if we'd only try.

Now, some of these old-time cures were wonderful. If you had a cough, take and go to work to make syrup out of chopped up raw onions—the more onions the better. Then you add sugar to the onions with a small amount of water, just enough to dissolve the sugar. Bring the syrup to a boil, then put it in a glass. If you have a bad cold or are coughin' a lot, just take a spoonful of the syrup and you'll stop coughin' right now. If the cough comes back, take another spoonful. You could even store this syrup for a while, maybe a week or two. Now, remember, in those days, we didn't have any refrigerator, so things could spoil fast in hot weather. We had an icebox, but it was used for fresh meat that we had to eat right away.

We used to mix up turpentine and lard to break up chest congestion. You rub it on your chest, right on the hide, and it broke up the congestion in your lungs. It was made by takin' hog lard that Mama would put in a pan and get real hot to sterilize and melt it. Then she'd pour some turpentine into the pan with the lard. Oh, probably about one-third of a cup of turpentine to about one cup of lard. Let it cool until it shapes up into a paste, kind of like the Vaseline we have now. Most generally, Mama would put it on us when we went to bed, but it could be used anytime.

I remember the first vinegar I saw. We bought it at a meat market in Cody that came in 50 gallon wooden barrels and had a little wooden faucet the storekeeper would open to pour you some. We used vinegar for cookin' and cannin' a lot. Vinegar is really good to calm an oozy stomach too. Take a whiskey shot of vinegar and it will straighten you right up. You won't believe this, but women are funny critters. My sisters would rinse their hair in it and swear that it helped their head. Us boys never used it; we didn't have time for vinegar. Maybe that's why I'm bald today.

Iodine and mercurochrome used to be the thing we'd use to stop infections and sterilize wounds. You can't find either one anymore. The mercurochrome could really sting so you knew it was workin' against infections. Least of all, that's what we thought back then. Now, drugstores still use it in prescriptions, but you can't buy it. They want to make money on it. Greed, greed, greed.

To prove my point, they took it away from us and then turned right around and let the salt companies use it for iodized salt. See what hounds there are these days?

In old-time drugstores, you could walk in and just ask for iodine, mercurochrome, or quinine. They'd just sell it to us. Most generally, the biggest thing sold in drugstores back then was candy, soda or other sugary stuff. Old time drugs were sweets, ha! We could buy envelopes and stamps there too. The first soda I ever had was not at a drugstore. It was made by Mama. The best root beer back then was just root beer extract and water. She could make a great root beer.

One of Mama's main medicines for both colds and lung congestion was, believe it or not, Vicks VapoRub, which you could buy at the drugstore. Vicks or Mentholatum is great at night. You can rub it on your chest, right under the nose, and always on the bottom of the feet at bedtime if you're really sick. This really helps small babies 'cuz Mama used it on all of us kids. Vicks can't ever hurt you unless you get it in your eyes. My Mama and Doris' mom used it. We used it on all our kids too. Vicks is a lot better than havin' to take prescription pills. I wonder when they'll take it off the shelves too so no one can get it again.

Now, the king of all medicines and the master of all 'em is Asafetida. Of course, you can't get it now, but it saved many a life back in the old days. I've already told you about how awful it smelled, but it was really powerful. It smelled so bad that no one would come next to you and you wouldn't stand next to anyone else who was wearin' that ball around their neck. I'm glad they took it off the market 'cuz it was such a terrible smell. Mama said that it stopped the most serious diseases. Anytime those illnesses showed up in Cody, everyone in my family had to wear that stinkin' necklace. But we all lived to old age and never had any vaccinations. I never had a shot until I was in the army. They made me take all kinds of shots. Every one of us had to, but I can't even name them now.

CHAPTER 9

Politics

OK, I'll start politic stories with FDR. I got a chance to meet FDR in about 1943 or 1944 on the parade grounds at Fort Lewis, Washington. We were sent on a convoy to escort President Roosevelt and Army General George Marshall from Tacoma to Fort Lewis and back to Tacoma. A military newspaper at the time, *The Stars and Stripes,* said red and blue army units were there that made up more than five hundred thousand soldiers. You couldn't see the end of them on that parade ground and many of them couldn't see FDR either. Marshall and FDR came there to review the troops and stayed quite a while. When they were ready to leave, about 35 of us .50 caliber machine gunners escorted them back to Tacoma. Before they took off in their big airplane, we sat on our half-tracks with full artillery. You know, I thought about it later, but any of us could have killed the president right then and there since there was nothin' to stop us. We all had live ammo and were armed to the teeth. FDR called each machine gun operator over, shook our hands while palming over to each of us a silver dollar, and thanked us for our service. I still have that silver dollar to this day.

FDR really had the humor. When we crossed the parade grounds, the 98th Field Artillery had their mules grazin' nearby. Those mules just took off buckin' and playin' and ran right by all the escort vehicles including FDR's vehicle. When FDR took the microphone and addressed the huge gathering of soldiers, he sure made us laugh.

He said, "I think my party has turned against me. Mules are the mascot for the Democratic Party and this bunch of mules act like Republican elephants."

He was a great guy. If anyone ever says anything bad about FDR, you need to ask them, "Is that is why they elected him four times?"

Back then, even some of the Democrats were angry that he had been elected four times 'cuz they wanted a chance to run for president. Then these Democrats got together with some Republicans and passed a law that presidents can only serve two terms. That happened after FDR died, I think.

I have a lot of respect for FDR. Let's look at what he did durin' the Depression for the senior citizens. One of the first things FDR did after he was elected was talk with Dr. Francis E. Townsend. You see, FDR beat Herbert Hoover during the election of 1932. Hoover had Dr. Townsend put in prison for startin' a civil riot when people gathered to support his ideas. So in 1933, FDR took office and was really concerned about the well-being of older Americans. The Depression was goin' full blast, and the old timers were really strugglin'—dyin' by the thousands, cold and freezin', hungry and sick. Dr. Townsend had a plan called the Townsend Plan where he wanted to give every American over 65 years old a payment of $200 per month, but every penny had to be spent to help the economy. No one was allowed to save this money; it was Townsend's idea to spend every nickel to stimulate the economy.

FDR said he liked the Townsend Plan, but he didn't like the name. So they came up with the name of Social Security. The reason FDR didn't like the Townsend Plan was 'cuz the U.S. government couldn't afford to pay all the old people $200 per month. So they agreed to let employers and employees contribute to the Social Security fund, which turned out to be a wonderful idea for the old people in America then and now.

FDR came from a very wealthy family, but he always looked out for the workin' man and the poor people. To me, a great leader is not a selfish man.

Over the years that FDR ran for office, I voted in every election. But after FDR was elected, I don't think any other presidential candidate, Democrat or Republican, ever cared about this country as much as FDR. If you had a chance to ask any old Republican who was alive in those days and they were truthful, they'd tell you the same thing. FDR was respected by members of both parties. FDR was elected hands down every time he ran. Can you imagine what this country would be today, if FDR hadn't led the U.S. during WWII? We'd be eatin' sauerkraut or rice.

It's interestin' to know that my granddad, Frank Lundie, worked for Teddy Roosevelt on his ranch in Dickinson, South Dakota. I think Granddad did ranch work for Teddy Roosevelt when he first left Canada before he made it to Wyoming.

Some of the most wonderful American programs in history were the Civilian Conservation Corps or the CCC. Young kids were shipped all over this country. They worked in forests, on highways, in cities, streets, anywhere the American people needed help. All the money the kids earned had to be sent home to help their folks and the economy. The CCC built the road from Trout Creek up to Dickinson Park near Fort Washakie. Other projects were done across the nation too.

The Works Progress Administration was another FDR project. They nicknamed it WPA. This program was designed to help the workin' man feed his family. It was also created as a nationwide project. The WPA made office buildings, built bridges, houses, roads, everything a community needed. The workers in this program were adult men and the federal government was their employer. WPA awarded grants to projects that built up communities and then the local projects paid the workers who in turn could take care of their families. Remember I told you about my workin' at Mammoth in Yellowstone Park? That was a WPA project. For example, 256 men were employed right there on that one project in Mammoth. Most of all the work was done by hand by the men. We didn't have the modern machinery that's around today.

Well, you know how politics are. Sometimes we just keep makin' the same mistakes. If the current government followed some of FDR's ideas and philosophy, it would line this country out right now. As far as I'm concerned, FDR is the only president we've had that worked for the poor people.

Well, this country is so divided now it's pitiful. It seems like we think more about the foreign countries and the UN than we think about this country. FDR always thought about the USA first. If the Japs hadn't hit Pearl Harbor, this country would never have entered WWII. FDR used to say and it was a good sayin' just like in a baseball game. The United States is home plate and if we don't protect home plate, then we lose the game. That's not true today 'cuz all our government is doin' now is thinkin' about foreign governments and helpin' the rich people or corporations. A good example everyone knows about is the Mexican border. We're not protectin' home plate when we let all these foreigners come into this country, take our jobs, spy on us, and you name it. We don't pay attention to it while so many people are always tryin' to come in to the USA so their kids can have a better life. I heard that the Chinese are takin' over Seattle 'cuz there are so many of 'em. I've always said that if someone talks like I talk, as an isolationist, it's a bad deal. But, today I'd rather be an isolationist than under one of those foreign governments. Wouldn't you?

We've lost every war and every military action we've been in since WWII. Now, listen here, it took us ten years to get out of Iraq and we're back in there again right now. It took longer than that to fight in Afghanistan and we're still there too. What are we doin' over in the Middle East? No one can tell me why we're over there. The only answer is to protect American interests and what is our interest except oil? But the government won't come right out and say it. Seems to me it's not in the U.S people's interest—it's strictly in the oil industry's interest.

Our government gives money to a country anytime they need it. We just give it to 'em. Whenever a bank needs a bailout, we give it to 'em. Whenever a corporation needs help, we give 'em millions. But we have to fight for every penny that goes to people right here at home. We have to get down and beg 'em, and that ain't right. We pay income taxes right through the nose. I can't understand how the government makes us beg to get some of our own tax money back.

I hope and pray that we don't lose this country. One of these foreign governments is gonna come in here and take the old USA. Then what will we do? If we got in trouble today, who's gonna come help us? Nobody! That's why, in my opinion, we should never be in the UN or this so-called world government. We're at the point right now with our government that, in my opinion, politicians are tryin' to rule the whole world and not payin' attention to the American home base.

When the economy is down in our own country, why do we buy everything we need from overseas? I'd like to know that. It's just givin' our economy away to foreign governments. The environmentalists are partly to blame too. There are so many environmentalists that get laws passed that industries can't do their jobs so they have to take their business overseas. That's how I see it. If you can buy everything that's made overseas, why can't we make it here at home? We did it before and we can do it again.

Now, we're all environmentalists. We all need water, air, a home, and food that make up our environment. So we're all environmentalists just tryin' to live in this crazy world. When water burns right out of the faucet, something is really wrong and it won't be fixed very quick. That's happenin' around this country' cuz of oil and frackin' industries. Water that burns? My Mama would never have believed it. They say the earthquakes are increasin' everywhere too 'cuz of all the holes we punched in Mother Earth. She's gonna have enough one day and flip us right off her back.

Politics are so complex. It's just like you go to bake a cake and pretty soon, 20 other women are there too. You can't get a cake baked. That's just how our government is now with all these other countries and corporations tellin' us how to run the United States. That's the God's truth.

I've voted my whole life as a Democrat. I'd be lyin' if I said I don't vote since I still vote in the general elections. The first person I ever voted for was Franklin Delano Roosevelt while I was in the army. I think 95 percent of the servicemen in those days supported our president. FDR loved this country and the people trusted him. That's why he was elected four times. Now nobody trusts the government—Republican or Democrat. They used to say, "United we stand and divided we fall." Well, we're sure as hell divided today. I'm worried about my grandkids and what this country will be like in the future. Everyone should be worried. We've all heard that God blessed America. It's a good thing God will bless us, since the politicians won't.

My family was active in politics in both parties. Uncle Bob was an active politician. He got a lot more active when he had a few snorts. Like my grandmother said, who was Uncle Bob's sister, at political meetings in the Long Hollow school house, Uncle Bob couldn't stand on the floor and speak. When he had a few snorts and was high, he needed to stand on a high place, so he'd jump on the table. Eventually, the table would fall 'cuz he was rantin' and ravin' but he'd just keep talkin'. He was very good at usin' profanity too. He'd get himself straightened up after the table fell and then he'd just clam up.

Once, the men all got together and dug a pit and sawed through a big piece of cottonwood that was made into a table for Uncle Bob's politickin'. Uncle Bob didn't know about the table or the pit 'cuz the ladies had gotten together and made a political quilt for the table. One side of the quilt was Democrat and the other side was Republican. Uncle Bob would stand on the Republican side since that's the party he belonged to. At the next political meeting, the quilt completely covered the table and when Uncle Bob jumped on it, he didn't succeed at bustin' it down like he always did. So he said that the damned Democrats must have made the table.

He said, "That's why you can't trust 'em. You never know if they'll stand up for you."

Back in those days, people didn't care what party you belonged to. No one held grudges back then. That's when our country was really united no matter what side of the quilt was showin'. Doggone it, yep, that political quilt was in the house we lived in at Cody, but nobody checked on it, and it got ruined 'cuz of the rain and mold. What a shame.

I thought I'd enter into politics officially when I belonged to the local AFL-CIO union, back in St. Helens where I was elected vice president. I was a shop steward and I was on the Grievance Committee where I represented the workin' men's side when it came to a grievance with the company. That's probably where I got started as active in politics.

When we came back to Wyoming, I ran for Fremont County Commissioner two or three times and got my ass beat every time. Me bein' a Democrat and Fremont County being ruled by Republicans, it took me a long time to realize I could never win a race in Fremont County. Even though I campaigned for office, there was no way I could win. Doris was always behind me and supportive, but she was too bashful to go up to total strangers and ask them to vote for me. She didn't have to do that 'cuz I really didn't want her to campaign. I was runnin' for office, not Doris. She wouldn't run for a race ever— she wouldn't even have walked for one.

Joking aside, I'm really disturbed by the current political situation. In my opinion, I think we've lost this country. We're no longer Democrat or Republican. Americans are all about greed now. We can watch the TV and see the governments of foreign countries, like China, buyin' up so much of this country that we're broke. When you turn over our economy to our enemies, like China, Russia, North Korea, North Vietnam, and Cuba, you have no economy left.

Now, think about what I'm sayin'. We have thousands of Americans without jobs and we ship manufacturing jobs to our enemies. That makes no sense to me. Those countries manufacture their products with slave labor and turn around to sell it in America at high prices as if it were union labor. These foreign governments have America on a wheel and we just keep spinnin' around, givin' 'em everything and they just keep takin' it.

Lundie Thayer, 2016, Lander, Wyoming, age 101 *(Karen King photo)*

THE WHITE HOUSE
WASHINGTON

March 25, 2015

Mr. Lundie P. Thayer
Lander, Wyoming

Dear Lundie:

Happy 100th birthday! We are delighted to send our warmest wishes as you celebrate this special occasion, and to thank you for your service and sacrifice.

Your story is an integral part of the fabric of our Nation, and over the course of a century you have witnessed the kind of tremendous progress that is possible when we work together in pursuit of a brighter tomorrow. We trust you take enormous pride in everything you have accomplished and in the ways your service has touched the lives of others.

Again, happy birthday. We wish you the very best.

Sincerely,

Michelle Obama

Birthday wish from President and Mrs. Obama, 2015 *(Lundie Thayer records)*

Copy of Lundie Thayer's birth certificate *(Lundie Thayer records)*

Lundie Thayer, age 99, by Wyoming highway sign about
his birthplace, c. 2014. *(Karen King photo)*

CHAPTER 10

Characters

I've known lots of interesting characters. One was Bill Abshire, who was part Seminole Indian. His folks originated in Florida. Well, Bill followed the trappin' trade as his business and for pleasure he liked his whiskey. You could say drinkin' was his sport. Bill used to come into Cody from Sand Coulee between Powell and Cody and the Montana line to sell his animal hides. He trapped coyotes, bobcats and anything else he could sell. After he got to Cody and got some money for the hides, he'd start bendin' his elbow and get pie-eyed.

There's a sad part about old Bill. He had a gray saddle horse and when he got pie-eyed he'd get on that horse and head right back to Sand Coulee. Well, Bill came up missin' and no one could find him or his horse anywhere. About thirty-some years later, they did find him.

A sheepherder was walkin' up the side of a washout and he looked down where he saw some bones all in a pile. So he went down to check 'em out. There, he found all of Bill's bones and his horse's bones too. I named my horse Pilot after old Bill's horse 'cuz he was such a great horse to take a dead-drunk rider right back to his cabin safely. Anyway, after all that time in the washout, the saddle had dried up and all that was left was the cracked saddle tree. The whole thing had shrunk over the years in the hot Wyoming sun and cold winters.

Bill was a really nice guy when he was sober. He wasn't an alcoholic all the time. He just drank when he came to town. One time, he got drunk in Cody and he had a run-in with the law. Two game wardens had gone out to his cabin and broke into it just as Bill was comin' back from checkin' his trap lines. Well, old Bill opened up on 'em with his rifle. He didn't aim to kill 'em, but it was cold as hell out and he wanted the game wardens to cool down too. He kept both of 'em from goin' back to their truck or into Bill's cabin. They went and hid behind the cabin, but Bill still wouldn't let 'em leave to find a warm place. Bill finally decided they had had enough, so he quit firin' at them. Both wardens ran to the truck and took off like the mill tails of hell. I don't know where that sayin' comes from, but it means really fast.

Eventually, the game wardens got the county sheriff and two or three deputies to go out to Bill's Sand Coulee cabin and pick him up. Bill didn't fight 'em when they put him in jail. In a day or two, they took him to the judge.

The judge asked the wardens, "Did you have a warrant for Bill's arrest?"

The wardens said they didn't have a warrant, but the sheriff said he had one.

Then the judge said, "You know it's against the law to break into anyone's house without a warrant. Why did you do it?"

The wardens said, "We wanted to confiscate evidence."

The judge replied, "You know it's against the law to break in anyplace."

The wardens said, "Yes."

The judge then looked at the bandages on their fingers, nose and ears where they had gotten frostbite when Bill held them back with his rifle.

The judge then said, "Now, looks like you've learned your lesson, so remember to always take a search warrant with you and never break into anyone's place without one. Case dismissed."

Well, that was the law and I think it still is the law today. Today's laws don't seem to matter, and the lawyers, judges, and courts just push their weight around any old way they want to. I sat in on Bill's hearin' and that was a good judge, but I can't remember his name.

Bill Abshire was involved in another incident that should have had the law involved too. Bill was in Cody and drunk, as usual, when he decided to buy a car. He didn't know how to drive, but that day he didn't know that he didn't know how to drive. That was when the law should have stepped up, but it didn't happen that way.

Seems that day Bill picked up his drinkin' buddy, Cy Foster, in his new car that was an old used Dodge with a canvas top and they headed toward Sand Coulee. Bill rolled that car over on Skull Creek which is a very interesting name considerin' what happened to Cy. When the car rolled, Cy's head got cut off. When a rider on a saddle horse found the wreck, Bill was sittin' in the sagebrush and Cy's head was missin'.

After a look around, the rider had to ride all the way back to Cody to inform the officials of what happened. Even with extra help, they couldn't find Cy's head until the next day. It was about a quarter of a mile from the wreck where evidently a coyote or wolf or mountain lion or some large animal had hauled it off and dropped it. For a while, people thought the reason the animal had dropped Cy's head was 'cuz the animal was drunk just from Cy's head bein' in the animal's mouth. Today they call them alcoholics. Back then, we called them drunkards. Cy wasn't a bad guy, but he couldn't go on without his bottle.

After that case was over, Bill came into Cody again to sell more hides and he proceeded to take his money to play his sport again. He started up drinkin'. He came up the middle of the street with his 30 x 30 rifle and told a guy, "The goddamned sheriff is in that pool hall. You go in there and tell him I'm out here waitin' for him."

The guy went in, but the sheriff said, "I'm not goin' out there. He's gonna try to shoot me," and he went out the back door instead.

Bill went on down the street laughin' and havin' his own little party since the sheriff didn't want to face him. Bill won that game of his sport.

But, Bill and Pilot lost the game of life, just what happens to all of us. People thought that Bill and Pilot had tried to cross the washout when it was plumb full of snow. When they started across the snow, it gave loose and they went down in the washout. I believe both man and horse suffocated in all that snow. The newspaper even said that the washout was 20 or 30 feet deep and snow filled the whole thing. That's the only thing people could figure out about why Bill and Pilot's bones were at the bottom of that washout all those years later.

Now, I'll tell you about another character. I was comin' down the street one day in Cody and my brother, Sid, drove up in his Model A pickup. Sid asked me if I wanted to work with him the next day, helpin' to move Yellowstone Red's sheep wagon. Sid was the boss then for Trout Creek Cattle and Sheep Company up on North Fork outside Cody. Yellowstone Red was hired to tend the sheep and Sid wanted to hire me to move Yellowstone Red's sheep wagon to the lambin' pens. I said yes without hesitation.

Sid said that we had to get an early start the next day 'cuz he wanted to eat breakfast at Yellowstone Red's sheep wagon since Red had the best sourdough in the whole world. Sid and I both wanted to eat some of Red's sourdough pancakes and, boy, did we. After we ate, we had to wash the dishes, so Sid sent me down to the spring to get a bucket of water. It was still dark outside and when I brought the bucket of water up to Red's sheep camp, Sid prittin' near shit his pants 'cuz the water was full of maggots. We found out the next day, that an old ewe had died just above the spring and the maggots fell into the water. I didn't know it then 'cuz it was still too dark.

Sid looked into the crock where Red's sourdough was and it was bubblin' like mad. We got to lookin' closer and saw all of 'em maggots in the sourdough too. You can't believe how good sourdough pancakes taste even with maggots.

Sid said, "Well, Pete, it's too late now to do anything different. They're already down the hatch."

Yellowstone Red came back in after tendin' the sheep to enjoy some hotcakes that Sid made for him too when Sid jumped him, "You know your sourdough? Well, it's got maggots in it!"

Yellowstone Red said, "A few skippers won't hurt ya' none." And then he ate every bite of those hotcakes too.

After Yellowstone Red was done with his breakfast, I hooked up the team, sheep wagon, and the trap wagon with all the gear and proceeded to move out.

Sid said, "Wait a minute. I want to tell Yellowstone Red somethin'."

We pulled up to where Red was tendin' some sheep. Now, I don't actually know what Sid said to Yellowstone, but I did hear Yellowstone Red say, "You guys go over there and sit in the sagebrush to talk to each other. I'll stay here and talk to my dog whose awful smart."

In other words, Red was callin' us dumber than his dog for bein' worried about eatin' "skippers."

I pulled Yellowstone Red's wagon about five miles and parked it for the night. The next day, we came to the lambin' sheds where Yellowstone Red was gettin' ready to lamb out. But old Yellowstone decided he'd go on vacation back to town with Sid.

Sid said to old Red, "You're gonna have to get a haircut and take a bath and put on some clean clothes before I pay you anything."

Yellowstone Red says, "I'm no longer workin' for you, so you're not tellin' me what to do no longer."

Sid piped up and said, "Mr. Yellowstone, that's the way it is," and we walked away.

Pretty soon, a representative of the prosecutin' attorney came up to us and said, "I want to talk with Sid. What's the deal that you're not gonna pay Mr. Yellowstone for tendin' your sheep?"

Sid said it again, "I'll pay him when he cleans up and not before. I'll give you the money and you can pay him yourself. But don't give him a cent until he does what I told him to."

'Cuz old Yellowstone Red stank like hell, the prosecutin' attorney said, "Does that include perfume too?"

Sid just said, "Suit yourself."

Yellowstone goes over to the Golden Rule Store to buy some new clothes, but Mr. Bratton who ran the store wouldn't let him in. Mr. Bratton didn't want Red touchin' any new clothes 'cuz he stunk real bad. So, Mr. Bratton says, "You can't touch any of these clothes until you take a bath."

I don't blame Mr. Bratton for lookin' out for his good clothes. Those were hard times and most men didn't take baths very often. But if a person was gonna buy some new clothes, they sure as hell didn't want 'em stinkin' and already dirty.

Next, Sid goes to see Curt Howell, the local barber in Cody. Mr. Howell said, "I will not cut Red's hair until he washes it and takes a goddamned bath! Most generally, when cowboys or sheepherders come into town, they get cleaned up before they get a haircut or shave. How old is he anyway?"

Sid said, "Well, old Red is pretty old."

Mr. Howell said, "OK then. I'll help the old guy with his bath."

Sure enough, Red got a bath, but he still didn't have any clothes to put on afterwards. Sid went back to Mr. Bratton and told him that Yellowstone Red was all cleaned up and ready for some clean clothes. Sid asked if he could bring Red some. Mr. Bratton agreed.

So Sid brought Red some new clothes and Mr. Howell said, "I've helped a lot of men take baths. But that's the first man I ever had to scrape."

Old Yellowstone Red was so dirty his undershirt just stood up by itself. He wouldn't change clothes at all unless someone made him.

I was just a kid and followed Sid around pretty much all day tryin' to get Yellowstone Red lined out and cleaned up. We finally got it done and Sid told Red to go over to the prosecutin' attorney's office and pick up his pay. Well, Red went over and got his pay and then came back to Sid and me and said the prosecutin' attorney wanted to talk to Sid. So, we go back over and that attorney held his hand out to shake Sid's and said, "Thanks. Old Red's a pretty good-lookin' guy when he finally gets cleaned up."

The last we heard of Yellowstone Red was when someone found him dead sittin' in a stairway in Billings, Montana. Everyone figured he died of old age and just went to sleep. He got the name Yellowstone Red 'cuz he was born and raised up by Custer, Montana, on the Yellowstone River. I felt sorry for the old man 'cuz he never had any family to look out after him, but he was a great sheepherder who could look out after sheep really good—a lot better than he looked after himself.

Now, let's go back for a minute to Curt Howell, the barber. He loved to take young boys and train them to box 'cuz when he was young, he was a professional boxer back east. Mr. Howell was a good enough boxer that at one point he was a third contender for the middleweight world champion title. He was a wonderful supporter of the Golden Gloves, which was a boxin' club for young kids.

We used to go in Mr. Howell's backroom at the barbershop where he'd set up a boxin' ring and we'd train there. He'd cut hair all day and then go home for dinner before he'd come back to let us kids in and train at night. That's why I still like the Golden Gloves from that day to this. I wasn't a champ or anything, but it learnt me how to take care of myself later on. The biggest purse I ever got was in Worland at a Golden Glove tournament when I was maybe twelve or thirteen. I won $5 for winnin' in three rounds.

I didn't go on with it, but I learned how to protect myself. I think every kid today should learn how to protect themselves; it's not gonna hurt any of 'em. I probably boxed in less than twenty matches for money. I was kinda lucky, though, 'cuz I think I won more fights than I lost, but I got my ears knocked down ever so often too.

Another character was Mr. Bulware who was a nice man that everyone appreciated. His job was to clean cesspools in Cody and keep the cisterns filled with water 'cuz there was no city water system or sewer system at that time. Another name for Mr. Bulware was Missouri Bill 'cuz he originally came from Missouri. There was a Mrs. Bulware too who was a very nice lady and us kids would give her some of our candy or licorice if we had any and she would always thank us so nice and sweet. That was her way, nice and sweet. Man, she could talk you out of things even if you didn't want to give her anything. Mama liked her too. Mrs. Bulware called Mama Flo and told her that she and Mr. Bulware were havin' a hard time makin' it. Mama always tried to help her too. Several years after Mrs. Bulware died, they found more than $50,000 in her kitchen cabinets. Mr. Bulware passed away before she did, but she had a sweet nest egg when she died. She sure did. But, she flew the coop and left her nest egg behind her.

Anyway, years earlier Mr. Bulware was cleanin' a cesspool when a young kid walked up to see what he was doin'. Sure enough, that kid fell in the cesspool. Imagine that if you can. Mr. Bulware had to jump into the cesspool to try to save the kid. It's a damned good thing that another man saw Mr. Bulware goin' into the cesspool, but he didn't know what for or that a boy was in there already. The man approached the cesspool and saw Mr. Bulware holdin' up the young boy so he wouldn't drown and helped both the boy and Mr. Bulware get back on solid ground. In those days, everyone helped anyone. That's the God's truth and it's the only way a lot of people survived. There was no greed like there is today 'cuz no one had anything to be greedy about. We just helped each other survive even if it meant haulin' 'em out of a pile of shit. It was the natural thing to do in them days.

We're goin' back, so I should tell you more about Tom Oliver too. Remember I told you about his wonderful dog, Jigs? Well, now, I'm gonna tell you another story. Tom came into Cody and got pie-eyed with Cy Foster. Both those drunkards got on top of the Cody Hotel and when the police told them to come down, they had other ideas. Since there was only one ladder to get on the roof, the drunkards started tearin' down the chimney brick-by-brick and throwin' those bricks at the police who were tryin' to climb up the ladder. Those two drunks whipped the entire Cody Police plus the Park County Sheriff's departments. They didn't have any bombin' planes or helicopters; they used what they found handy and what they could get. That day, they got bricks. When Cy and Tom were finally off the roof, they were escorted to jail right away. What's really comical about this incident is what happened to Sid.

Tom worked for my brother Sid sometimes and when Tom ended up in jail, the judge declared that he was going to fine Sid for the bail money to let Tom out.

Sid said, "You can shove it. He's not workin' for me right now. Can't you see he's on vacation?"

Well, the judge didn't think Sid was right on that point, so he said, "I'm gonna fine you too, cuz you won't pay Tom's bail."

Now, that's how stupid they were back in those days and how the law didn't make any sense to lawyers, judges, juries or common folk.

The Park County jail was always full 'cuz there were a lot of drunkards around town comin' in off the range from real hard work and ready to kick up their heels. The judge and the law tried to move the prisoners out as quick as they could 'cuz they knew there'd always be more. Since it was the Depression, there were plenty of hoboes there too.

Sid told his attorney, Milward Simpson, about what the judge had said to Sid and what Sid had said to the judge.

Milward asked Sid, "You told a judge to shove it?"

Sid answered, "Yes."

Milward then told Sid, "OK. I'll help you push it in."

Not really, I just made that part up to make you laugh. And you did laugh, huh? Anyway, it ended up that Tom got out of jail on good behavior and no one had to pay any fines.

Now, Milward Simpson was also the announcer at the Cody Stampede in them days. He used to open each evenin's rodeo and performance by sayin', "I'm wild and wooly and full of fleas. And I've never been curried above the knees. But, I'll make it into Cody for the next stampede. Let 'er buck!"

Another sayin' he used was, "Come on, all you rounders, if you want to raise hell. Here come the girls from the Cody Hotel with chopstick stockings and high-heeled shoes, with a package of smokes and a bottle of booze. Let 'er rip!"

Now, chopstick stockin's were what the high-falutin' gals wore with their high heels. The socks were loose weave and only came to about the middle of the calf of the leg. That's why they were called chopsticks.

People really liked Milward's sayin's 'cuz they'd clap and clap and clap. He really knew how to make the crowd excited, bein' quite the PR man. Now, imagine the father of a U.S. senator from Wyoming, sayin' such things every night to a crowd.

Earl Tennyson was another Cody character who liked his drink. He decided one night that he wanted some chicken for dinner, so he took out to steal some hens from the Park County Sheriff who was named Joe Freeburg. Well, Joe's dogs started barkin', so Joe goes out to see why the chickens were squawkin'.

At the chicken coop, Joe asked, "Who's in there?"

The chickens piped up and responded, "There's no one in here but us chickens."

Joe drew his gun right when Earl came chargin' out of the chicken coop and knocked Joe down. The gun went off and shot Earl smack-dab in the ass.

Even though Earl was taken to court for tryin' to steal chickens, Joe wouldn't press charges 'cuz he didn't intend to shoot him and figured that was enough of a fine with a bullet in his butt. A fine behind, so to speak. Ha, made you laugh again, huh?

My granddad, Frank Lundie, was the Northern Wyoming U.S. Marshall. Granddad and the Southern Montana U.S. Marshall delivered Big Nose George to the Wyoming Territory Prison in Rawlins. My understanding is Big Nose George's hide, or part of it, is still on display at the museum they made out of the old Wyoming Territory Prison. It's only something I heard; I've never seen it myself.

Well, Big Nose George was a bank robber and murderer all over Colorado, Wyoming and Montana. All this was before my time, but some folks have told me they saw that tanned hide. Big Nose George must have been a big asshole too.

I knew Archie Campbell, who was part Shoshone Indian and is buried at Fort Washakie Cemetery. One day, I was comin' home from cleanin' up the shoemaker's shop and Archie asked me if I had any money. I told him yes and he asked me if I wanted to be his partner.

Me, being a dumb-ass kid, asked, "Doin' what?"

Archie said, "I'm goin' into the rabbit business."

So I jumped at the chance to start a business and be a partner for only 50¢,

Archie told me to go over to the Cody Trading Company and see if they would give us a couple of pasteboard boxes. So I got the boxes and we headed out of town. He walked to a house outside Cody where Archie knew there were rabbits. The man who owned the rabbits was sittin' inside, lookin' out the window and watchin' Archie reach in the rabbit cages then put 'em in the boxes.

Yep, we walked home with those rabbits that started our new business. But, we hadn't even gotten them out of the boxes when Joe Freeburg showed up.

Joe said, "Archie, you take those rabbits and put 'em right back where you got 'em."

Archie said, "Come on, Pete."

Joe piped up and said to me, "You stay home, young man. Archie, you take those rabbits back one at a time."

Archie took all seven of those rabbits back one at a time and each trip was more than a quarter of a mile one way. That walkin' sobered old Archie up and when Freeburg knew the rabbits were all back where they belonged, the rabbit owner decided not to press charges against Archie.

By that time, Archie had sobered up and he said to Freeburg, "Am I free to go?"

Freeburg said, "Yes, but before you go, give Pete back his 50¢ partnership fee."

It was a 50¢ piece I had and I could always use it or give it to Mama. Honestly, I didn't know those rabbits weren't Archie's 'cuz he'd told me they were his. That's what drinkin' does for people. Archie was actually a pretty good guy, but the drink makes lots of people crazy, liars and thieves.

Archie, Joe Chavez and Frankie Tillman were all Shoshone Indians that sheared sheep all over the country with my brother, Charlie. One year, they decided to go to West Yellowstone in Idaho to the rodeo 'cuz all three of those Shoshone guys could really ride horses. Well, the bronc that Archie drew to ride was really a good buckin' horse. Archie rode him solid, but durin' the ride, Archie hit the horse over the head with his hat. The judges disqualified him for that and announced that was why Archie didn't win first place. It was against the rules to hit the animals in that race, but, man, animals were always bein' hit outside that rodeo and everywhere else.

Charlie and all the men had taken me along with them to the rodeo and when we decided to leave, we couldn't find Archie. We looked all over hell's half acre and still couldn't find him anywhere. Joe thought Archie had taken off to Idaho with another friend. There wasn't much else to do but go home without Archie. As Joe walked by the old Chrysler convertible we were all ridin' in, he heard a knock. When Joe opened the trunk of the car, there was Archie who had crawled in there to have a sleep, but he locked himself in too. Finally, we all made it on back to Cody.

Two or three days later, Archie went into the Cody Trading Company and told Clark Saunders who was a clerk there, "Do you have change for a twenty?"

Clark said yes, and counted out the change. Archie grabbed the money and ran out of the store thinkin' he'd pulled a good one. Well, they caught Archie an hour later. He said, "I just asked if he had change for a twenty. I didn't tell him I had a twenty to give back in trade."

Again, the charges were dropped against Archie after he returned the money.

Jakie Schobe owned the Cody Trading Company and he wouldn't file charges against Archie 'cuz he loved watchin' Archie ride broncs. In fact, Jakie usually paid Archie's entry fee to the Cody Stampede. Not all Cody characters helped each other like Jakie did Archie.

Some people didn't like one another at all and fought all the time. One of them was Ernest Peterson and his enemy was Mr. Ingram who ran the dairy in Cody. They didn't get along at all. One of 'em milked cows and the other raised pigs. I don't remember which happened first, but this is what ended up. Ingram's dog had a litter of pups and Peterson's cat had a litter of kittens. Well, the pups ended up in Peterson's cistern and the kittens ended up in Ingram's cistern. I don't know who dumped their litter first, but Ingram took Peterson to court. Peterson accused Ingram and Ingram accused Peterson. The judge ruled tit for tat and told them both to cut it out. I went to that hearin' too and it was a simple case of 'em gettin' back at each other.

Peterson and Ingram were both good friends of my family. One night, my folks, Peterson and some other people, were playin' High Five, a card game. They started to discuss religion durin' the game and it came up that Jesus Christ had died.

Ernest said real serious in his Swedish accent, "I didn't even know he was sick."

The whole place busted out laughin'. It still kind of tickles me with all these religious nuts these days.

Elmer Adams lived all over the place but was in Cody at one time. He was quite a character too. Elmer wanted to rent a little tin shack that Mama owned. He asked her, "Can you rent me that tin shack?"

Mama said, "No. It used to be a chicken house. Not fit for people to live in."

Well, Elmer told Mama he'd give her $100 a month for the place.

Mama said, "No, I've got to have $200," thinkin' he'd never pay that much for such a place.

Elmer agreed to the $200 and Mama let him move in, knowin' that he didn't have $200 and she didn't expect him to.

She told him, "You'll need to clean out the place before you move in."

Well, he couldn't sweep out the place. He had to shovel it out before he went back downtown to get his few belongings. Those poor souls, Elmer had very little in life, but here he came in an old Ford truck. He told Mama that he had a contract haulin' coal in the truck.

He was probably a better businessman than we have politicians now days 'cuz it cost old Elmer more to haul the coal than he got paid. That's the way our government operates right now, exactly like old Elmer who used to have to bum his groceries to keep his coal-haulin' business goin'.

Everyone helped old Elmer 'cuz he really should have been in an institution, but they didn't have any back then. He was harmless, which is very different from our government today.

After WWII, my sisters Nellie and Myrtle had another story about Elmer. My family had come from Oregon to visit our Wyoming family again when we heard about Elmer's visit to my sisters. Seems he pulled up in some old car that had a pretty good-sized trunk in the back.

He told my sisters, "Guess what I have in the trunk?"

My sisters couldn't begin to guess what crazy old Elmer had in that car.

Elmer told them, "Nope, you have to guess. I'm not tellin' you."

Well, they guessed and guessed and couldn't come up with the right answer. Finally, Elmer told 'em, "I'll surprise you."

He opened up the trunk. Lo and behold, there was a woman in there. She was alive and as silly in the head as Elmer. My sisters were totally shocked when Elmer told them that woman was his wife.

He said, "I'm takin' all you ladies to dinner tonight."

So they all went out to eat, probably at the Cody Café and had a fine meal. But when it was time to leave and pay the bill, Elmer had no money. So Nellie and Myrtle had to foot the bill. Nellie said, "I think it was all worth the laughs."

That's another way Elmer was like today's government. They fool you into givin' 'em somethin', but don't tell you the truth. That's our government up and down right now. They pay people $20 per hour and then turn right around and take $19 of it away. Our government is run today by the billionaires and the millionaires. The only people the government looks out for is the corporations who have all the money they need in the first place. The government is only using the common people to play the old shell game, just like old Elmer used to do.

Now I'll tell you about Wayne Schobe, who was the adopted son of Jakie Schobe. While we were livin' in Cody, Wayne would come to our house to visit and we'd get to tellin' ghost stories. Back durin' the Depression, we'd tell ghost stories 'cuz life was real scary and ghost stories made us feel better. Wayne would sit wide-eyed and listen to every word.

Now, it's the God's truth that we had some turkeys that used to roost in cottonwood trees right next to our gate. At night, when the moon would come out, the gobblers gobbled and made that crazy sound like cryin'.

Well, Wayne was comin' up our way to hear some more ghost stories. He'd already heard one of the ghost stories we told about some guys who were hung from the cottonwood trees on our place. We also told Wayne that if he ever heard any noise around those cottonwood trees, it was those hung guys' ghosts comin' back. Wayne was scared 'cuz he had to go in and out of our place every time right by those cottonwood trees if he wanted to hear more ghost stories.

Sure enough, one moonlit night, Wayne was comin' to hear the ghost stories and the gobblers gobbled. When Wayne heard 'em, he took off runnin' to our house. He hit the front door, never stopped to knock and tore that door to bits. Wayne landed in the middle of the front room floor.

Since we weren't expectin' company at all, let alone like that, we all got a bit spooked. Bugs jumped on top of whoever had landed in our front room before he ever knew it was actually Wayne.

Wayne said, "Those guys have come back! They made a real chokin' noise as they came after me!"

That sure was enough excitement for the night. No one told any more ghost stories that cold night.

Wayne went home and told Jakie, his stepdad, what took place.

Next morning, here come a man to our house named Albert Staggs with a brand new door in the back end of his buggy. Jakie had sent us a new door to replace the one Wayne broke up. Back in those days, people took responsibility for their own actions and for the actions of their kids. We never called the sheriff about those minor things 'cuz we could take care of things ourselves. We all knew what was right and wrong. I'm not sure anyone knows what's right and wrong these days.

Another famous Cody character was the man who the town was named for. Now days they call him Buffalo Bill. I never knew him personally, but like everyone, I knew of him.

Mama used to take half of us kids on the buggy into Cody to get supplies. When we got to town, all us kids had to stay right with Mama. She never let us go by the Irma Hotel 'cuz she knew that Buffalo Bill was always drunk and he'd sit on that front porch of the Irma. Later on, I heard that he was usually dead-drunk sittin' there. When Buffalo Bill left Cody, I don't know where he went, but some people said he went back east and died. Well, there's three places where Buffalo Bill is supposed to be buried. One is in old Cody, another is in Kansas, and another place is called Lookout Mountain in Colorado. Who knows where he is really buried? When you become an alcoholic, you can land up anywhere dead-drunk.

Two other characters lived in Cody. One was named Magpie Jack and the other was named Ed Tulley. Sid and I went into Past Time Pool Hall in downtown Cody when Magpie Jack and Ed Tulley were sittin' together, both of them prittin' near sound asleep. Well, Sid was always a character too who was tryin' to pull somethin' over on those two guys.

With Magpie and Ed snoozin' in their chairs, Sid decided he'd pull Magpie's hair and blame it on Ed Tulley. Man, the fight was on. Magpie weighed into Ed while Ed was still asleep. Sid and I just stood there and watched the show. They went to Knuckle Junction in a hurry and put on quite a show until Sid stepped in between them.

Sid said, "That's no way for friends to treat friends."

And the fight stopped. Sid never told anyone who pulled the hair first and caused the fight.

Ed Tulley lived up South Fork on a ranch. Sid sold him a team of horses; one was about eight inches, two hands, shorter than the other. Sid told me to lead the team out and make sure the short horse was on the side of the hill a little to make them look like they were even-sized. When Ed bought the horses, he hooked them to his buggy and drove 'em home.

Later, Ed said to Sid, "You know, Sid, one of them horses I bought from you is shorter than the other."

Sid said, "Well, they matched up when you bought them and you saw them with your own eyes."

Ed said, "I know, but I don't know what took place with this short one. You know something? This team is about the best team I've ever owned."

In them days, if you dealt in horses, you always had to wheel and deal. So Sid won that one. But Ed, you can bet your life, was always layin' for Sid to get even. Those old timers came up through life in really hard times and they always had to manage business even if it was sellin' sheep shit or tradin' short horses. Everyone in their right mind needs to appreciate how people survived back then.

There are two other characters I'll tell you about. One was named Rex Rice and the other was Barney Nelson. They both liked their whiskey to no end. One day, George Heald chewed Barney out for gettin' drunk.

Barney said, "I don't have to take that from you! I quit right now."

Mr. Heald said, "You can't quit 'cuz you owe me $25."

Barney came back. "As soon as I get the $25 paid back, I'm quittin'."

That same evening, Barney borrowed another $5 from Mr. Heald to get more whiskey. I tell you the truth, Barney had a mouth that looked like he was always suckin' on a whiskey bottle. His lips were naturally curled.

On my way to deliver some groceries to Mr. Heald's sheepherders, I killed a coyote, then skinned and hung its hide outside my camp to dry. Lo and behold, I saw someone drive up to my camp. Sure enough, it was Barney and Rex and they took my hide. Well, there was nothin' I could do about it. In about a week, a hide buyer showed up to buy the sheep hides.

I told the buyer, "There's three sheep hides I've got for you. By the way, did you buy a coyote hide from Barney and Rex?"

The buyer said, "I certainly did and gave them $5.50 for that hide."

Mr. Kurtz was the hide buyer's name; a Jewish man who knew how to be Jewish.

I told Mr. Heald that someone had stolen my coyote hide and sold it to Mr. Kurtz. Then I pointed right at Barney and Rex. Old Barney just stood there with his whiskey bottle lips, but he couldn't deny I was tellin' the truth.

I said, "I saw 'em take it and I know how much Mr. Kurtz give 'em for that hide."

Well, Mr. Heald had a habit of sayin', "Judas Priest," if anything went wrong. Sure enough, Mr. Heald looked at Barney and Rex and said, "Judas Priest. Do you boys have anything to say about Pete's coyote hide?"

Rex and Barney just looked at each other and finally said, "Yeah, we took it."

Mr. Heald responded, "Rex and Barney, you owe Pete $2.25 each for that hide. I'm deductin' it off your pay. Barney, at this rate, you're never gonna be able to quit. You owe me $32.25."

That was a fortune in those days. I was workin' full time, 24 hours a day every day, and got $30 a month. Barney and Rex were only gettin' $25 a month. I don't think Barney ever did quit 'cuz he liked his whiskey and he couldn't stay sober long enough to pay back Mr. Heald.

Barney was a cowpuncher for young George Heald when I was a packer for two sheep camps up on the forest reserve. One day, I went to Barney's camp and he told me, "I want you to bring me a quart of whiskey."

I told him, "You write out your order and I'll present it to Mr. Heald."

Barney said, "No, I can't do that. This quart of whiskey is just between you and me."

I told Barney, "The hell it is. There's no between."

Barney said, "I quit. You can take these cows and shove 'em."

I told him, "Those 52 miles back to Cody is gonna be a long walk."

Barney said, "You're crazy. I'm gonna ride my horse."

I told him, "Whoa, back up. I'm in charge of all livestock on this mountain for Mr. Heald. I've decided you're walkin' back to town or you have Mr. Heald buy you that quart of whiskey and not me."

Barney pointed his finger at me and said, "When I come off that mountain, I'm quittin'."

He never thought he'd owe Mr. Heald that much money. But he did.

Those guys were real characters. Between Barney quittin' all the time and him and Rex drinkin' whiskey all the time, it's a wonder we got any livestock taken care of. On some weekends, those two guys would be so blasted they wouldn't show up to work 'til Monday mornin'.

I can remember Mr. Heald saying, "Judas Priest. They'll be here Monday."

Now, there was a lady character too. Her name was Mrs. Bloom.

One day, my granddad said, "Lundie, I'd like you to take a saddle horse and four other head of horses down to Mrs. Bloom. I bought some pasture from her. You know where she lives?"

I said, "Yes."

So I saddled a horse and got the other four horses then headed toward Mrs. Bloom's. The wind was blowin' like the mill tails of hell. My saddle horse was plumb gentle until a tumble weed got caught in his tail and he bucked me into the dirt.

My granddad was followin' me in the old Model A pickup and he headed out to catch my horse.

Granddad always gave me encouragement and when he returned my horse to me, he said, "Lundie, you gave that horse quite a ride, but he's quite a buckin' horse too."

Of course, here I am, holdin' on to my hat against the wind and the old horse is mopin' along until that tumbleweed hits his tail. I didn't have time to even breathe before I was on the ground.

Well anyway, we got to Mrs. Bloom's place and turned all the horses in the pasture before she invited us into the house. There was a dead turkey, feathers and all, lyin' on the table. Mrs. Bloom goes over to the bird and gently pulls a feather off his head sayin', "He's not ripe enough to eat."

My granddad was a very clean man and when Mrs. Bloom asked us if we were gonna stay for dinner, he said, "No, we don't have time for that turkey to get ripe and I'm in a hurry."

After that, we thought Mrs. Bloom was a little touched. Later, Tom Oliver told me that people in Lapland, I don't even know where that is, always waited until the feathers of any fowl could be pulled out real easy before they cooked it. Sounded to Granddad and me that Mrs. Bloom couldn't have been in her right mind. But, we were wrong.

That old bitty was really smart. Here's how I know. Mama and Bugs went to Mrs. Bloom's to buy some hay. They bought it 'cuz it looked good in the stack but come to find out she had hidden foxtail grass in the center of the stack and went around the outside with second cutting alfalfa. She was real tricky.

The next day, Bugs and Sid went to get a hayrack of hay from the stack Mama bought. When they got on top of the stack, they saw the foxtail and came home without any hay. They told Mama what was happenin'.

Mama said, "You hitch up my buggy and horse. I'm gonna see that old bitty."

Mama came back home with the $50 she'd given for that stack of hay and Mrs. Bloom had told her, "I don't blame you, Mrs. Thayer. I was gonna burn that stack anyway. I sold you the wrong stack."

She was such a rascal. One time, she hired me to put up hay for $1 a day. She asked me if I would take part of my pay in trade. I went home and told Mama that Mrs. Bloom was tradin' my work for turkeys or ducks or chickens.

Mama said, "In trade?"

Sid was sittin' there too and Mama told Sid to tell me the facts of life.

Sid piped up and asked, "She doesn't need another hand, does she?"

Oh boy, Mama really flipped her lid then.

One time, Mrs. Bloom had hired a couple of Swedes to work for her and they worked for nothin' but trade. Come to find out, Mrs. Bloom was also tradin' her body as well to get ranch work done. She was quite the business lady, always and all ways busy.

In the summer, she ran her ranch under the same terms, but in the winter, she took her hired help to mine coal from her mine and sell it. Mrs. Bloom would herd sheep too in the winter and eventually became very well-to-do. To show you how well-to-do she was, she rode into Cody on an old sorrel mare with men's winter underwear on over her dress.

The banker would come out to hold her horse while she took the winter underwear off before she went into the bank. Sure enough, her dress looked really good, considerin' she'd been horse back. She really had a good system to keep herself lookin' good.

Us young boys would sit at the bank waitin' for someone to hire us. The bank was like our employment office 'cuz we'd take any work we could get. We used to tell Mrs. Bloom plenty of BS like how beautiful she was. Mrs. Bloom would take us to the beer parlor and buy us enough beer to split right down the middle. No one ever got a full beer, not with Mrs. Bloom.

Her husband was another Laplander and just as crooked as she was. He knew what she was up to all the time too. Mr. Bloom asked me to help him deliver some potatoes. He had ten sacks of potatoes and each sack weighed one hundred pounds. He'd deliver to Cody stores and restaurants. We took one sack into the Cody Café and for my pay he ordered me a T-bone steak and one for him too. When we got done eatin', he told the waitress that he had no money, but he would give her one hundred pounds of potatoes and call it even.

The waitress said, "That's fine, Mr. Bloom. I'm gettin' low on potatoes."

I tell you, they were some funny people and would never tell the truth right out front.

A couple of other characters I'd like to tell you about were named Beaver and Beaverhammer. Honest that was their names. I was crossin' a piece of land once with Beaver, my sheepherder. Lo and behold, here came a guy out of the bush who was wild and wooly as any sheep could be.

He stuck his hand out to Beaver and said, "How are you, Mr. Beaver?"

Beaver said, "I'm fine, Mr. Beaverhammer."

I was sittin' on my saddle horse, thinkin' I was listenin' to two idiots 'cuz they just kept shakin' hands and sayin' that greeting over and over again.

Finally, Beaver said to me, "You catch Mr. Beaverhammer a sheep."

I was workin' for Mr. Heald, not Beaver, and I thought those two kooks was gonna steal a sheep from Mr. Heald.

I told Beaver, "If you want a sheep, you catch it yourself 'cuz I'm not stealin' any sheep from Mr. Heald."

Beaver said, "Wait until I see Mr. Heald. You'll be fired right on the spot."

So I took Beaver on up and across Beaverhammer's property when Mr. Heald rides up.

I see him talkin' to Beaver and then he said to me, "I'd like to have you, young man, make Beaver think he's the head cheese around here 'cuz if I had to pay him off, we'd both be out of a job. I'll take the blame. I should have told you that when we cross Beaverhammer's land, we have to give him a sheep. I didn't tell you that so I appreciate you lookin' out for my interests, but a deal is a deal. I'll fix it up with Mr. Beaver."

That's just another example of how honest some people were back then and how most of them kept their word. Of course, there are examples of how dishonest people are too like the Blooms.

Another important character I'll tell you about was named Kid Nichols. He lived up South Fork outside of Cody and his hobby was raisin' thoroughbred Hereford cattle. His wife didn't like him comin' in the house with cow manure on his feet or smellin' like a cow, so he went and had a nice little white house built right in the middle of his cow corral. He loved his cows, maybe more than his wife. I'd help him round up, brand, or whatever had to be done, and we always cleaned up and ate in that little white house. It was sure a nice little home.

Kid Nichols loved to tell stories too that entertained us young boys. One day, we were sittin' on a rail outside the bank that we called our employment office and the banker came out. Now, this is the God's truth, the banker told us, "One of these days, I'm gonna have that rail taken down. Then where will you roughens sit?"

Kid Nichols jumped down from sittin' in the center of us boys and said, "Mr. Markham, when you have this rail taken down, I'm gonna have it put inside the bank 'cuz it's colder than hell outside on this rail. And I'm gonna make you into a shoeshine boy."

Mr. Markham about fainted and said, "Lord, have mercy on my soul. I didn't know you, Mr. Nichols, was sittin' there."

Kid Nichols repeated, "The day this rail is removed is the day you'll become a shoeshine boy."

The stories go on about Kid Nichols. Here's another one. Yellowstone Park Rangers shot Kid in the hip so he limped on one leg. They shot him 'cuz he killed an elk, not knowing that he was inside the park when he did it. Well, Kid took off on his one leg, made it all the way across the park and caught a freight train box car to head back east to New York.

While he was sittin' by a fire one night, he put two sticks across one another and it gave him an idea. The two sticks were stronger crossed over each other than single sticks lined up next to each other. That's how Kid Nichols got the idea of patentin' a product that he called plywood—'cuz he piled those sticks together.

Then he went to work and got two guys to finance his idea. They each put up $500, but Kid still needed a little bit more money, so he bought back their shares just payin' them interest and eventually developed a patent on his own. I think he said he made one cent per square foot all over the United States no matter where the plywood was manufactured. Imagine how much money he earned. He had two accountin' firms, one in California and the other in New York City, but he never forgot where he came from. Kid came from workin' class people in Cody. He became a very wealthy man who never forgot the underdogs. He told some pretty good stories to us men, but I can't tell you any of those stories, you bein' a lady. Kid was a mighty fine person with some wild stories.

Art Cooley was another fine man from Cody. He was Chuck Cooley's dad and they were both interestin' characters. Mr. Cooley, Art, had a team and wagon that we went around Cody with cleanin' ash pits.

Now, an ash pit was a four foot high mound of cement that was hollowed out to hold ashes after whatever was burned. My job for Mr. Cooley was to clean out the ash pits since I was a boy and he was a man who couldn't fit back in there. I'd go in and push the ashes toward the door and then Mr. Cooley would take the ashes out and put 'em in the wagon.

You can't believe the way those older men treated us younger boys. One funny day, we were ridin' down the street in the wagon and Mr. Cooley says, "You go over there and ask that lady if she wants her ashes hauled."

I goes over, knocks on the door and a beautiful lady answered. I asked, "Do you want your ashes hauled?"

She looked at me then said, "Young man, to haul my ashes, it will cost you $1."

I still didn't get what she was talkin' about, so I said, "I'll go tell Mr. Cooley what you said."

She said, "You do that."

When I got back to the wagon, Mr. Cooley was laughin' so hard he couldn't talk, just slappin' his knees and laughin' loud. I found out years later that the house I went to was a house of prostitution. The reason I know that is 'cuz Art's son, Chuck, told me, since old Mr. Cooley played the same trick on young Mr. Cooley.

I have a few stories on Chuck Cooley too. He rode a little mare up to the livery stable there in Cody and went to put her in the corral when he saw a man laid out on the manure pile.

Chuck asked Sid, "What's that man doin', lyin' on the manure pile?"

Sid said, "He's dead. When I get time, I'm gonna bury him."

Chuck ran and got on Betty Jean, his little mare, and took the reins hittin' her where the foal sucks and headed home. Sid told me Chuck was about scared to death.

A half hour later, here comes Art Cooley who said, "Now, Sid, Chuck told me what you did. We've been good friends for a long time and if you killed a man, do not bury him in a manure pile."

Finally, it dawned on Sid what the deal was.

Mr. Cooley went on, "We have to find a way to make it right."

Sid said, "I've got a way. Let him sober up. I forgot to tell Chuckie that the man was dead drunk, not just dead. I didn't put drunk in there."

Mr. Cooley broke out laughin' again, sayin', "That's the easiest murder that's ever been solved."

Snipes the Sugarhead is quite a character too. He'd go around Cody, on the main street, pickin' up cigarette butts. One day, we took a full cigarette and tied a real light thread around it when we saw Snipes the Sugarhead comin'. First thing he did was spot that cigarette. Old Bob Dare was way down the street and he had the end of the thread tied around the cigarette, so every time Snipes the Sugarhead tried to reach the cigarette, Old Bob would inch it further away. That went on for prittin' near a whole city block. Still makes me laugh and Bob got to laughin' so hard he just gave up.

In the summer, Snipes would run a little truck farm right in the middle of Cody, sellin' lettuce, carrots, onions, radishes, and you name it—he'd sell everything he could grow. I worked for him off and on by cuttin' ends off the vegetables. Snipes would pay me one-fourth of a cent for six onions or carrots. So for a penny and a half, I topped six vegetables. Times were tough, but we sure had good, pure food and lots of practice with arithmetic too. Snipes would sell six onions for three cents, and he'd bundle six carrots and sell them for three cents too. Snipes was a real hard worker. I can still see him hoein' his garden even when it was prittin' near dark.

Snipes would find cigarette butts anywhere he went and put the leftover tobacco in a cigarette paper and have a full cigarette to smoke eventually. He was smart that way in savin' as much money or tobacco as he could. People called him Snipes 'cuz he'd pick up all the cigarette butts to make him a full cigarette. We called butts snipes back in those days. I don't know why he was called Snipes the Sugarhead, but everyone liked him. I know one thing that Mr. Markham told me about Snipes. "He's after the money and you can bet he got it."

Let's talk next about Tex Thomas who was another character. He used to pull cars up the hill to Buffalo Bill Dam 'cuz they didn't have enough power to make it themselves. Tex was a bull shittin' cowboy. When Doris, the boys, and I came from Oregon to visit Cody, I took 'em to see the Buffalo Bill statue. When we got there, here was old Tex standin' with his horse, Monty. He immediately looked at my car's license plates and he thought for sure we were a bunch of dudes. He knew we were dudes when my kids wanted to know why he had a six-shooter on.

Tex told them, "I'm here for one reason—to make sure you all are safe. Sometimes, Indians will come up over the hill and I have to shoot 'em."

I recognized Tex, but he didn't know who I was.

One of my boys asked him, "Can I see your gun?"

Tex told him no 'cuz he never let his gun loose since that was a very dangerous area. Then one of the boys up and asked if they could ride Tex's horse.

Tex said, "That'll be up to your folks. Sometimes, I let boys and girls get on my horse. I charge them 25¢ for each ride."

Of course, our boys wanted two quarters to go for a ride. We told them OK. Tex sat them one at a time in the saddle and led them around the statue all the time ravin' about bein' an old Indian fighter. His job was to protect the Buffalo Bill statue 'cuz all the Indians hated Cody and Tex had to protect all the visitors.

Well, I got sick and tired of hearin' his BS so I told him, "Mr. Thomas, if bullshit was music, then you'd be a whole brass band."

He said, "Who are you? How do you know me?"

I told him I was raised in Cody and I knew him and Mrs. Thomas who ran the hospital.

Tex said, "Yeah, the Mrs. is still at the hospital, but who are you?"

I told him I was Lundie Pete Thayer and shook his hand.

Tex said, "Just forget what I said about all that stuff. A man has to do anything to make a livin' even if it involves lyin'."

Believe it or not, my wife and the boys all believed his stories.

Doris said, "Why didn't we just drive away? You didn't have to call him a brass band. You could have told us later."

I told my Dude, "I can only take so much crap like that when it's all BS."

She said, "I believe his stories and so do the boys."

Tex had a stage coach and he'd bring the real dudes, not Doris, over to Cody from the depot which was across the Stinkin' Water River—Shoshone River. He was a real roustabout and full of BS with all the tourists and anyone else who would listen to his stories. By the way, Tex charged every person 35¢ per passenger to bring 'em to Cody. He made good money doin' those trips—that was a lot of money at that time. Just think, bringin' three dudes over was $1.05 and I used to work all day on ranches just to earn $1.

Tom Donley had a small ranch in Meeteetse. He asked me if I would stay with his boy for a week while he went back east for some business. I agreed, and so did another kid named Orville Kolinsky. Mr. Donley said OK to both of us and told us if we needed to get to town for anything, just crank up the old Ford pickup that his boy, Tom, knew how to run.

Well, bein' three hoodlums wantin' a joy ride, we all wore out our arms crankin' that old Ford but couldn't get it started, so we just gave up on startin' it. Instead, young Tom told us he'd show us how to shoot a pistol. Well, it was a German Ruger pistol and a real treat for us.

You know what he did? He took that pistol and held it real close to his eye to get a good aim, and when he pulled the trigger, it recoiled. I thought he was dead. It knocked him a little bit cuckoo, but not plumb cuckoo. What scared me was the blood. Here we was about ten miles from town with no way to get back to Meeteetse.

To show you how stupid young boys can be, we cranked that pickup just once and it took off.

Young Tom got behind the steerin' wheel since no one else could drive and headed to town. He drove the whole way with one hand on the wheel and the other hand on his bleedin' eye.

We got into Meeteetse and couldn't find a doctor or a drugstore open. I think the adults who saw young Tom were as scared as I was.

Finally, an old lady came to look at the eye and said, "I'll stop the bleeding, but you have to take him on to a doctor in Cody."

She stopped the bleedin', but the eye looked like a black and blue baseball since it swelled up so much. A man had a buggy in the livery stable and he took Tom into Cody where the doctor put a few stitches in his eye. Orville and I stayed in Meeteetse with nowhere to go, no food, no money, and no idea what to do next since we couldn't drive that Ford.

The same old lady who patched up Tom's eye told us that she'd fix us some sandwiches and let us stay in her barn. Next morning, she fed us a real nice breakfast and said, "We should know how that boy comes out pretty soon."

Sure enough, the next morning, here came young Tom and the man with the buggy. Young Tom drove the Ford back to the ranch— this time with both hands and a big swollen eye. He went on to be fine, never got blinded, just had a scar on his cheek.

Someone told old Tom about the incident when he came back to check on his boy. Finally, old Tom took young Tom to Cody to get the stitches out. Even though young Tom got hurt while we were babysittin', old Tom gave us $5 a piece for our good work watchin' out for his son.

My granddad ran the Pilot Ranch for Henry Sale who had a storekeeper named Bob Burns, not the famous poet, but his name was really Bob Burns. Mr. Burns would order vanilla every time they needed supplies bought from the Meeteetse Mercantile.

My grandmother asked my granddad, "Did Mr. Burns order any more vanilla? It figures he ordered more 'cuz every time I need some vanilla, he never has any. When he does have it, he only gives me one bottle."

So Granddad got to thinkin' and checkin' the books. Sure enough, every order had vanilla which came in 24 bottles to a case. Mr. Burns was in charge of all the orders for the sheep business, the cow business, and the ranches, including the Pitchfork Ranch that Mr. Coe owned. Granddad asked my grandmother if she would take care of orderin' all the vanilla and he'd have Mr. Burns come get the vanilla directly from her.

One day, Mr. Burns said he put in an order for vanilla, but Grandma asked, "Well, Mr. Burns, what are you gonna cook?"

He answered, "I'm not gonna cook nothin', but vanilla is good for the soul once in a while."

So Grandma gave him a bottle anyway.

Then Mr. Burns told Granddad, "You're goin' overboard with that vanilla orderin' shit. I'm the storekeeper and Mrs. Lundie is doin' my job."

Granddad said, "Mr. Burns, you're drinkin' that vanilla and I know it. Aren't you?"

Mr. Burns nodded yes.

Granddad said, "My wife will keep doin' the vanilla orderin'."

Once in a while, Grandma would send vanilla out to the camps with Mr. Burns. Sure enough, that vanilla never made it to the camps but lightened Mr. Burns' soul before the sheepherders could get any. Finally, to solve the mess, Granddad ended up deliverin' all the vanilla to all the sheep and cow camps himself.

Mr. Ahlberg was a fine shoemaker who came to Cody from Sweden where he was told in Swedish to never let a black person sit behind you or near you 'cuz they would stab you or cut your throat. Well, Mr. Ahlberg was headed for Ohio to meet up with another Swedish shoemaker he knew there. While he was on the train, two black guys tried to sit down behind him. Mr. Ahlberg jumped up and showed them his knife, which ended up with him in custody. Mr. Ahlberg told me himself that he couldn't speak English, but he wasn't gonna let those people sit behind him 'cuz he didn't want to have any throat cut, 'specially his.

After a day or two, the authorities found someone else who could talk to and understand Mr. Ahlberg. Come to find out, the authorities knew Mr. Ahlberg's concerns and told him they would release him if he'd get on the train again and head to Ohio even if black people sat behind or in front of him.

Funny how the color of someone's skin can change how you see 'em. Probably happens to every human when they see someone different than 'em. Good thing flowers and most veggies don't have eyes since there are so many colors among plants and they can all live in the same garden.

As a kid in school, I used to go to Mr. Ahlberg's shoe shop, pick up all the leather scraps and clean the shop up on Saturday afternoons. During the week, if I had time, I'd stop in to Mr. Ahlberg's shop just to hear his little song. His little song was really simple. It went, "Hummidy dum dum dum," that's it.

I asked him why he sang that all the time and he said he was singin' to his sewin' machine. Hummidy was the start of the machine, and dum dum dum was when the needle went down and came back up. He said that song made his machine work better. For my labors around his shop, Mr. Ahlberg gave me a dime every Saturday afternoon. He was a really nice guy—just him and the Mrs., no children.

Another wonderful man me and the rest of the Thayer clan knew real good was Jim Kelley who ran the livery stable in Cody called the Keystone Barn, which was about where City Hall sits right now. One day, I was sittin' out on a bench and I always liked to talk with Mr. Kelley.

When he walked by, Mr. Kelley asked me, "Son, are you good with your dukes?"

I told him I thought I was pretty good.

He said, "You see that boy comin' down the street? If you knock the shit out of him, I'll give you a dollar."

I asked, "Mr. Kelley, why do you want me to do that?"

He said, "Every time he comes by here, he calls me an old gray-haired SOB."

I said, "OK, that does it. I'll give it whirl. I'll try him."

Mr. Kelley said to me next, "Well, if he knocks you out, I'll give you a dollar anyway. I just want him to know that I have a friend."

The kid's first name was Bleucher. I can't remember his last name now, but I knew him when I was only about ten or twelve years old.

Bleucher came by and looked right at Mr. Kelley and said, "How you doin', you old gray-haired SOB?"

That's all it took. I was on top of him like hell fightin' a bear. I don't know whether Bleucher knew what was takin' place until I finished workin' him over good. That was the best thing I ever did 'cuz I really liked Mr. Kelley and told him, "You keep your dollar 'cuz I bet he doesn't come by here again after that fight."

Mr. Kelley said to me, "A deal is a deal. Here's $2—one for the fight and the other dollar 'cuz you told me to keep the first one."

Mr. Kelley had a herd of black-faced buck sheep. There wasn't too many black-faced buck sheep in the country at that time. He'd rent those bucks out to people who had a few sheep so they could expand their herds to black-faced sheep. Mr. Kelley did quite well in that business.

Once a month, the lazy Cody postmaster would let Mr. Kelley take his bucks and graze them on the post office lawn so the postmaster didn't have to mow it. I'd heard about the lawn, so I figured I could earn a dollar a month from the postmaster to herd Mr. Kelley's bucks on the post office lawn. That was a good deal for both of us.

Mr. Kelley wouldn't take nothin' off nobody. As I've told you before, Bill Abshire was quite a drunk. One day, he went over to the Keystone Barn and threatened to shoot Mr. Kelley with his 30 x 30.

Mr. Kelley told Sid, "Bill Abshire must never come in here again and threaten me with his rifle. If he does, I'll blow his brains out 'cuz I won't take his shit or anybody else's."

Once, I was ridin' between Cody and Chipmunk Gap while Mr. Kelley was headed out to his homestead at Chipmunk Gap. I asked him, "What are you doin' out here?"

He told me that his horse had got out and he was lookin' for him. Well, by this time, Mr. Kelley was really old and was ridin' that horse—the one he was lookin' for. Mr. Kelley told me he was gonna stay at his cabin that night and find that horse tomorrow 'cuz he was sure the horse would come home. Sure enough, Mr. Kelley came in the next day about two o'clock, tellin' Sid that he had found his horse.

Sid asked him, "How'd you find the horse?"

Mr. Kelley said, "Oh, he was out there at the ranch."

Mr. Kelley was always nice to kids, but he didn't care much for adults. Every Thanksgiving and Christmas dinnertime, my mother and my grandmother would cook a big meal for the old people on the Poor Farm. When Mr. Kelley was put on the Poor Farm, he'd be among the old people when they came to eat. I think Mama and Grandma gave Mr. Kelley extra food 'cuz they knew how nice he had been to us kids.

During prohibition time, the county even allowed Mama some money to buy, if she could find it, some whiskey for the old timers who liked their liquor. Granddad even loved those holiday meals and a little snort every now and again. I used to sit in the back corner and was never allowed to say anything 'cuz Mama told me to just listen. I swear if my mouth had been opened and the sun was out, I'd have a sunburned throat 'cuz those old gentlemen had some really wild tales. Those people were totally honest, so I knew they were tellin' true stories that were really wild. That's how it was back then. Be honest or be known as a liar. Pretty simple, eh? Think of what the old people have now—nursing homes and no whiskey. I'm never gonna be in a nursin' home. Nope, not once. I'm tellin' ya the truth.

Bugs, my brother, and Mr. Kelley and a few other old-time sheepherders worked for the YU Ranch at Meeteetse. During shearin' time one year, a Mormon sheep-shearin' crew was shearin' YU sheep. Bugs and Mr. Kelley were sittin' out on the steps of the mess hall when a man came up to them.

The man by the name of Mallett had been drinkin' and said to Mr. Kelley, "I hear that you are a good gun fighter."

Mr. Kelley replied, "There's a lot of things you can hear."

Mallett said, "Listen here, feller, I'm gonna walk around this building, and when I get back, you better have your gun ready because I'm gonna blow you to hell if you don't."

Mr. Kelley asked Bugs, "George, what should I do?"

Before my brother could answer, Mr. Kelley said, "I'll just play it safe," and walked over to his horse, reached in his saddlebags and pulled out a pistol.

Sure enough, Mr. Kelley came back and was just ready to sit down next to Bugs when Mallett yelled, "Here I am!" and started to raise his gun.

Mr. Kelley fired at Mallett, and he blew the thumb and one finger off of Mallett's hand. Mallett went to Cody to get his hand patched up. That ended his sheep shearin' for that season.

But, the sheriff came out a few months later and arrested Mr. Kelley for first-degree murder. Mallett had gone to Billings to see a doctor who saw that blood poisonin' had entered his whole system and he died.

At the trial for Mr. Kelley, a funny thing happened. I'm not sure if Milward Simpson or Ernest Goppert defended Mr. Kelley. Anyway, one of them got up before the jury and said, "Mr. Kelley, you didn't intend to kill Mr. Mallett, did you?"

Mr. Kelley responded, "Goddamn right, I did. I meant to blow his brains out!"

As it happened, the judge ruled that Mr. Kelley must be out of his mind to say such a thing and told the jury, "All this evidence I've heard and all these people favorin' Mr. Mallett were lookin' through glass. The only witnesses were lookin' through glass and couldn't see what really happened."

That was the statute back in those days that you had to see something with your own eyes, not behind any glass. I'm not sure if that's the same law today, but it was in those days. Bugs' testimony was the only one accepted because he was sittin' in the open, outside the building and saw everything that happened. The jury came back in favor of Mr. Kelley and he was acquitted.

I heard it for myself at that same court proceedin' that Mr. Kelley had killed seven men in Spokane, Washington, at a loggin' camp. Every time that was brought up, the judge would tell the prosecutin' attorney that he couldn't bring that information to this case, meanin' he couldn't convict a man on current charges for past actions.

The judge went on to say, "I've already checked on those murders and Mr. Kelley was acquitted of each of them, so look at this case only."

Mr. Kelley was again acquitted, but he was sure charged with a lot of murders. He was a really nice guy with some pretty rugged luck.

Some other characters that had some rugged luck back in those days were called saddle tramps. They were men that would ride into your camp and steal anything they got their eyes on. Sometimes, they'd go to a ranch, get a job, and they would case out the place. After workin' a day or two, they'd steal everything the ranchers had. Now days, people call thieves highway robbers. Back then, we had the same type of people but didn't call them horseback robbers, we just called them saddle tramps.

Century celebration

Singer Kevin McNiven, left, sang songs in honor of the 100th birthday of Lundie Thayer, third from left, at a celebration held April 11 in the Monarch Room of the Pronghorn Lodge. Also pictured are Thayer's niece Ingrid Teuscher and friend Karen King. About 50 people gathered to celebrate Thayer, who was born April 8, 1915.

Photo by Anne McGowan

Lundie Thayer's 100th birthday celebration, 2015.
(Wyoming State Journal photo)

Lundie Thayer, age 98, Trout Creek, Wyoming *(Karen King photo)*

CHAPTER 11

Advice

Here's some advice for a long life. I've been raised on good common food. I never drank much and only smoked a tiny bit when I was young. I've always kept busy. A lot of the names, events, information and dates I told you were handed down to me. Maybe I got some of it wrong, but I tried my best. Tellin' the truth helps a person live long too.

EPILOGUE

    Lundie planted his last full garden a year after we drafted *Lundie's Stories* in 2015. By 2016, he also chose to plant more evergreens on the north border of his property. Two plantings were needed and supplied after Lundie told the producers it was their fault for not advising him about the altitude limits. Lundie babied those trees, and when only five of the 25 showed signs of survival, he had me in the spring of 2018 cut out the dead and brown. The six blue spruce trees were thriving that were given to Lundie in 2014 on a street in Riverton by a stranger who wanted Lundie to take them so he wouldn't have to haul them to the dump. The spruces were nearing ten feet tall, but the new fir and pine were weak. Lundie didn't like those trees. That's why they wouldn't grow is my opinion on the matter.

    The prairie roses Lundie dug up along his driveway in April of 2017 became his pride and joy. The boundaries of his once verdant garden still burst with horse radish, rhubarb, and wonderful pale pink peonies. But the prairie roses were his new pets that he kept near his porch so he could watch them grow, bloom, and fade.

    Like all living flora and fauna, Lundie faded. At the end of January 2016, Lundie fell in his kitchen. When I found him with a bloodstained shirt and pants, he was very pale. I asked, "Did you fall?"

Yes, he nodded.

"Where does it hurt?"

Lundie tried to lift his arm to point to his ribs but winced in serious pain.

"We have to go to the hospital to see if you broke anything."

Above his adamant protests about calling an ambulance, I managed to get him in my car.

Three cracked ribs were shown in the X-ray and the ER doctor demanded Lundie spend the night in the hospital.

"I promise I'll take you home tomorrow if the doctor says everything is OK," I told him.

"You better keep your promise," Lundie replied.

He went home the next day and healed with the three-month support of his eldest son who tended carefully to his dad's needs.

Lundie said, "That boy of mine is a pretty good cook. But, his housekeepin' is piss poor."

Generally, strong health was given to Lundie for more than ten decades. Prostate issues, like most men his age, made Lundie take only one pill a day that he called "my birth control pill." His last and biggest complaint was weakness in the legs. Although he'd do leg lifts, deep-knee bends and stretches while sitting on his couch, he was slow to step and very cautious to walk by planting hands and feet on solid surfaces before any other movement.

Because he didn't have the balance to winterize his lawn mower and rototiller, he asked me to help see that his equipment was safely stored in his shop in 2017. During every step of those chores, he guided me, making sure I did exactly as he said. His eyes were always quite keen and I was always pleasantly surprised when he asked me to do things for him since he trusted very few humans unlike his solid trust in many animals.

"If I'm gonna die, let's get 'er done. I can't stand this cripplin' around," Lundie said with disgust.

"You're never going to be 80 or 90 years old again, Lundie. You need to be proud that you take only one pill a day and that your mind is clear. Sure, you're pretty much deaf, but you never listened very well anyway," I teased.

"You're quite the brainwasher, you know. I know I'm just an old man, but I sure wish I could do half of what I used to," he responded.

Partner, Lundie's wonderful cat who could show everyone how ladies sleep in the morning, died in the spring of 2017. Lundie called me on a Sunday afternoon to say that his Partner was real poorly. He thought maybe it was a broken back since Partner wouldn't walk or stand. When we got to the vet's office, Partner was weak but purring because Lundie was loving on him. The vet couldn't identify any broken bones, swelling, or open wounds from the X-rays but thought that IV fluid and antibiotics might help.

We were leaving Partner in her care for the night when Lundie noticed a tiny drop of blood on the exam table. The vet shaved Partner's neck and found the dreaded two stab sign of a rattler's bite. She would keep IV going and call us in the morning.

Partner didn't make it. We collected his body and buried him at Lundie's place near the lumber piles where Partner always found lots of mice. I cried; Lundie wailed. He told me months later that he was still hunting for that blasted snake that got his Partner.

There are people who choose to share their lives with animal partners rather than human family members. Lundie's children urged him for decades to move closer to them, but Lundie wouldn't leave Doris and his youngest son's graves, his animals or his trees. The oldest son visited every year to help with garden harvest or preparation, firewood splitting or stacking, and other chores. He also stayed with his dad when Lundie broke his ribs. His daughter came to Cody in 2009 when Doris was ill and died. The other son came to visit Lundie in 2015 for a few days. A niece from Powell and her husband joined Lundie and I for many years, cleaning Cody family graves. After the cleanup and redecorating, Lundie would host the group to lunch at the Irma Café. Yes, the same place Lundie was told to avoid as a child because an intoxicated Wild Bill Cody would be there.

He rarely drove after his 102nd birthday, although he told me he still went every week to "see Mark and Mom" at Mount Hope Cemetery, their final resting places above Lander, where Lundie would one day rest as well.

Keeping busy was the key to Lundie's longevity. He still changed the oil in his rigs, sharpened his mower blades, and sorted seed catalogs that he reviewed carefully until he was 97 years old but didn't order seeds or seedlings very often like he had done in his prime. He continued his creative efforts by inventing the Lundie Loop, complete with prototype and plans to manufacture. We had discussed doing test drives at local schools to see how kids responded but settled instead with letting visiting kids or adults take a spin. Lundie had designed and made a prototype of Lundie Loop entirely of PVC tubes of varying lengths and diameters with the goal being to push the handle like a vacuum cleaner at different speeds either forward or reversely and keep the bottom loop turning without dipping to one side or the other.

Lundie would scamper around his living room to demonstrate the proper functionality of the Lundie Loop and give directions for others like, "Turn left," "Reverse," and "Around the table." Many children enjoyed Lundie's last invention, but Lundie did not enjoy the prospect of establishing another business, paying for another copyright and marketing the toy. I suggested he work with video game producers who could package their sedentary computer games with a Lundie Loop that required all users to get up and move after two or three games rather than sitting for long hours.

Lundie commented, "That's what makes America so fat. They all just sit, especially the kids, in front of computers."

Lundie never owned a computer and rarely watched TV except his favorite, *The Lawrence Welk Show*, on Saturday nights which was broadcast on the one and only channel Lundie received.

In his final months, he would sit on his davanaugh listening to his own thoughts. When a faraway look would cross his face, a smile would crack ever so slightly and he'd pipe up, "Did I ever tell you about that old sorrel that Uncle Bob had?"

Then more stories would be told.

He subscribed to the local county newspaper for years and would invariably engage in political questions and discussions every time I visited. I'm quite sure he also started political discussions whenever anyone else visited him in person or on the phone. His lifelong interest in politics prompted him to stay fairly informed on international, national, regional and local events although his news sources were very limited.

He'd tell me, "Listen to what I tell you. This country is on its way to communism. Republicans and Democrats are the same thing. Greed is the new name for politics now. Lies and corruption, sex scandals and pornography is everywhere. Does anyone know what's right anymore?"

Lundie's views on this country's military were far more negative in his last years than when he served during WWII. He'd repeat, "We're all over the world with no one left to guard home plate. FDR always told us to guard home plate. Why do we have to save the world when we won't fix our own country? Bring all the soldiers home and put them to work fixin' the roads, bridges and infrastructure."

His optimism and pride in the military shrank further when questions regarding Russia involvement in the 2016 presidential election surfaced. "Anyone who thinks Russia is helpin' this country is a fool. They're only helpin' themselves to this country."

On Memorial Day weekend of 2017, I drove Lundie to decorate the Cody and Meeteetse graves of his relatives. Mr. Bennion and Lundie's niece, Ingrid Thayer Teuscher, joined us for the drive and cleanup with another of Lundie's nieces. Lundie was irritable and nothing made him smile that day. Later, I wondered if it was because he somehow knew it was his last visit to his Cody and Meeteetse homeland and the cemeteries that held his family members. His hearing loss made it difficult to hold conversations in bustling environments and he remained distant from Mr. Bennion the entire day, missing out on those interesting stories about restoring antique cars, genealogical research and resources, as well as stories of the Meeteetse area that his family knew. Alas, Lundie didn't get to know his cousin or the many family members that Ingrid had recently connected with through DNA results.

During his last weeks, many kind characters came into his life. Neighbors would bring him sweets and treats. Waitresses were astounded at his mobility and quick wit when he'd tell them, "That'll be sanitary," which simply meant "OK". Nurses and doctors during regular checkups were enthralled with his clear mind and memories of days forever gone. The medical staff was equally amazed when he quickly revived after arriving via ambulance in the Lander hospital emergency room on Thanksgiving, November 22, 2018. Earlier, I tried to deliver to him fully-loaded turkey, fixings and pumpkin pie plates that I knew he would so enjoy but found him non-responsive and stone-cold in his bed.

A team of hospital professionals gathered around me while sitting by his bedside on November 27, 2018, to say there was nothing left to do. They had contacted his family and told them they did not expect Lundie to make it through the night. 24 hours previously, the family had confirmed plans with a local nursing home to transport Lundie there when the paperwork was completed. I thought, "Lundie always said he would never go to a nursing home and he'll make absolutely sure he doesn't."

I held his hand and read to him from a Will Rogers book, although I doubted he could hear me above the noise of various machines.

Occasionally, I'd call out, "Lundie, I love you."

He would always hear that and reply, "I love you too... Karen Thayer... I mean Karen King."

When I kissed him goodbye, I knew it was the last time. I told him like I always did when we parted, "I'll see you soon."

A last bit of advice Lundie shared was regarding trust. He had often said, "Never trust anyone, even family. They're the ones that will hurt you most." Despite my asking Lundie's children to come to Wyoming to say goodbye, none came. They have their own stories to tell and reasons why they wouldn't come to put their father to rest. I know he was a one-of-a-kind character and I will always be grateful to have known him as my forever friend.

Lundie died during the early morning of November 28, 2018, in the Lander Hospital. On December 5, 2018, he was laid to rest in Mount Hope Cemetery next to Doris and Mark overlooking the beautiful Lander valley. A few people gathered to pay their respects. A Shoshone great-nephew sang a journey song. A Shoshone niece offered the Lord's Prayer. An Arapaho great-great niece and two non-native neighbors told stories. I read the following poem.

Oh, Lundie Thayer

KK King

12/3/19

Oh, Lundie Thayer,
I hope I see you over there.
Above the clouds,
Away from all the pain.
Oh, Lundie Thayer,
I wish you happiness and joy,
To you, the best,
God grant a peaceful rest.
Oh, Lundie Thayer,
These mountains call your name aloud.
Oh, Lundie Thayer,
The rivers hold your jokes.
Oh, Lundie Thayer,
My world was better with you here.
But now you're gone,
The memories will live on.

Printed in the United States
By Bookmasters